I Want to Talk With my TEEN About

LOVE, SEX & DATING

BY

DR. KARL & SHANNON WENDT

Standard
P U B L I S H I N G
Bringing The Word to Life
Cincinnati, Ohio

Credits

I Want to Talk With My Teen About Love,
Sex & Dating
© 2006 Standard Publishing, Cincinnati,
Ohio. A division of Standex International
Corporation. All rights reserved. Printed
in China.

Credits
Produced by Susan Lingo Books™
Cover by Diana Walters

13 12 11 10 09 08 07 06   9 8 7 6 5 4 3 2 1
0-7847-1898-9

Contents

Introduction

Got a nickname? We both do. Kind of.

I (Shannon) frequently give presentations to schools on topics related to sexuality, but students don't always remember my name. More than once a student has seen me in public and called out, "Hey, everybody, look over there—it's the ... um ... the ... the Sex Lady!" Great. So I'm *The Sex Lady.* At least they remember me.

I (Karl) produce a daily counseling radio program called *60 Seconds to Think About.* Imagine my surprise when one of Shannon's staff (in a Christian sex-education ministry, mind you) dubbed me *The 60-Second Guy!*

Can you laugh about such topics with your teens? Sometimes laughter is the easiest way to approach a topic that you would rather avoid. *I Want to Talk With My Teen About Love, Sex & Dating* will guide your family through the dangers of sexually transmitted diseases, the pressures of the media to look and act certain ways, tough questions about dating, and how to find the "right one" for a lifelong mate. There are also hard topics, like boundaries, dating dangers, and forgiveness, that need serious thought and prayer. We even share myths about relationships and sex—and how to avoid jerks (and jerkettes)!

We pray that *I Want to Talk With My Teen About Love, Sex & Dating* will make the task of talking with your teen about tough topics easier and more comprehensible. It should. After all, it was written by The Sex Lady and The 60-Second Guy.

Karl & Shannon Wendt

Where Do You Stand?

Walking alongside teens as they move through adolescence, dating, and sexual urges and changes is difficult, thrilling, and confusing—all at the same time! This questionnaire will help evaluate your own strengths and weaknesses and where your own values and philosophies fit in. Circle the number that best corresponds to your answer. Then add up the total of your answers and check out the How You Scored box! (Retake the quiz after reading the book to see if your score changed!)

OPTIONS

❶ Strongly agree

❷ Agree somewhat

❸ Disagree somewhat

❹ Strongly disagree

I WORK ON MY OWN MARRIAGE, LOOKING FOR OPPORTUNITIES TO GROW IN UNDERSTANDING AND COMMUNICATION.

❶ ❷ ❸ ❹

I BELIEVE THAT MOST MEDIA DEPICTIONS OF MARRIAGE AND SEXUALITY DISTORT GOD'S DESIGN AND INTENTION.

❶ ❷ ❸ ❹

I AM CAREFUL ABOUT THE SEXUAL CONTENT OF WHAT I VIEW ON TV AND THE INTERNET.

❶ ❷ ❸ ❹

I SET ASIDE TIME TO TALK ABOUT LOVE, DATING, AND RELATIONSHIPS WITH MY TEEN.

❶ ❷ ❸ ❹

I AM AWARE OF CHARACTERISTICS OF TYPICAL TEENS IN THE NEW "MILLENNIAL GENERATION."

❶ ❷ ❸ ❹

I AM AWARE OF MYTHS ABOUT SEX, LOVE, AND DATING COMMONLY BELIEVED BY TODAY'S YOUTH.

❶ ❷ ❸ ❹

I ALMOST ALWAYS TREAT MY SPOUSE WITH RESPECT, COMPASSION, AND UNDERSTANDING.

❶ ❷ ❸ ❹

I KNOW WHAT SEX EDUCATION IS TAUGHT AT MY TEEN'S SCHOOL AND IF IT FITS OUR VALUES.

❶ ❷ ❸ ❹

I HAVE FOUND PASSAGES IN THE BIBLE THAT GIVE ME DIRECTION AND HELP IN TALKING WITH MY TEEN ABOUT SEX.

❶ ❷ ❸ ❹

I'VE BEGUN DISCUSSING TOUGH TOPICS SUCH AS PORNOGRAPHY, CONTRACEPTION, AND ABORTION WITH MY TEEN.

❶ ❷ ❸ ❹

HOW YOU SCORED

10—20 Give yourself a pat on the back! You seem to have a healthy perspective on love and relationships and work hard to keep the lines of communication open, even on tough topics. You seem aware of the climate of today's teen and how it influences the emotional and relational development of your teen. The way you treat others will be positively reflected in your child and will serve him well throughout his life!

21—31 Your relationships have experienced ups and downs. And although you work hard to communicate with your teen, you would love to make your communication more consistent and effective—and you'd love for your teen to learn from the mistakes you've experienced!

32—40 You may have been hurt in past relationships and are eager to help your teen avoid pain. You long to be closer to your teen and to improve your communication. You'd love for your teen to have a better, healthier life than yours—and today is the beginning of that journey!

It's Not Too Late

So you're the parent of a teenager. Congratulations! You are in for the ride of your life! No matter how many (or how few) of your parenting goals have already been accomplished, it is not too late to make a difference in your child's life.

Avoid myths about teens and parents.

True or false: *Parents are out-of-touch, disinterested dorks, and teens are rebellious, spoiled, drug-using brats.* False! Those gross generalizations inaccurately describe the average teen and miss the heart of most parents. Let's take a closer look at the truth about today's parents and their teens.

Welcome the good news.

key point
DON'T
BELIEVE
BAD STEREO-
TYPES.

It seems that every time you turn on the TV, you're bombarded with images portraying today's youth as hormone-driven, binge-drinking, disrespectful kids who skip school to play video games and have their tongues pierced. It was just a few short years ago that *Newsweek* magazine stated, "Kids today … [are] just no good. No hardships + no cause = boredom, anger, and idiocy." But new research says that those negative stereotypes are wrong! Many experts now see signs that make us believe today's youth are turning a corner—for the good!

key point
DON'T
IGNORE
THE GOOD
NEWS!

MYTH 1: TEENS ARE STUPID.
In the 1990s, aptitude test scores rose within every racial and ethnic group.

MYTH 2: TEENS ARE PESSIMISTS.
9 out of 10 teens describe themselves as happy, confident, and positive.

MYTH 3: TEENS ARE SELF-ABSORBED.
Today's teens are team players who believe in cooperative group activity.

MYTH 4: TEENS ARE DISTRUSTFUL.
Over 9 out of 10 teens say they trust and feel close to their parents.

MYTH 5: TEENS ARE NEGLECTED.
Today's teens are the most watched-over generation in recent memory.

"Over the next decade, the Millennial Generation will entirely recast the image of youth from downbeat and alienated to upbeat and engaged—with potentially seismic consequences for America."
—Neil Howe and William Strauss

You may ask, "If this group of teens is so positive and dynamic, why won't my kid quit back-talking and mow the lawn?" The answer is often not so simple. Relationships can be complicated, and this book is

Millennials (born in or after 1982) differ in many ways from Generation X. This new crop of teens and young adults appears to place a much higher value on teamwork, achievement, and good conduct.

designed to help sort through some of the most common diffi-culties and improve parent-child communication. After all, if we can't even talk about what happened today at school, how can we hope to discuss dating, love, or sexuality? Don't worry. We'll get there. But the journey won't be without challenges.

Today's teens are really aware!

Even though this new generation has so much going for it, there are reasons to be concerned. Civic spirit and test scores may be up, and crime and risky behaviors may be down, but most kids today believe that oral sex is not sex, and STD cases have skyrocketed in alarmingly young populations. On the heels of some very promising tendencies comes challenging sexual news about this generation that mandates our involvement.

key point
TODAY'S TEENS ARE SAVVY.

Today's parents need to realize that kids are connecting verbally and physically faster—and earlier—than previous generations.

Kids today talk about and know more about sex than any previous generation. But it is also true that a surprising percentage of what they *think* they know is actually *mis*information. Much of what today's teens hear and learn is from each other. And though even they realize that their own peers are a questionable source of information (at best), locker-room and mall-walk conversations still have a powerful impact on teens' sexual beliefs and values.

BOOMERS	GEN-Xers	MILLENNIALS
prefer "black & white" thinking	value a grey world	comfortable with paradox
follow moral values	value no absolutes	prefer "black & white"
idealistic	cynical	optimistic
value people's words	value people's actions	value people & community
live to work	work to live	live to know

(Gallup Survey Results, *The Seven Cries of Today's Teens*)

STOP & CONSIDER...

This teen generation will one day be running the nation. The country may be in better hands than we've thought.

This creates an especially difficult situation for parents. We are faced with the challenge of opening an extended dialogue with our teenagers on the supercharged topic of sexuality (which none of us is very comfortable discussing anyway). And we also have to share our hopes, beliefs, dreams, and sexual values with teens who think they know more than we do about love, sex, and dating. (We'll see later that in some areas that may even be true.)

> *"Our generation isn't all about sex, drugs, and violence. It's about technology, discovery, and coming together as a nation."*
> —Mikah Giffin, 17

Unfortunately, some of what teens believe they know is riddled with half-truths and outright lies.

Never has our input as parents been more necessary—or more difficult. The millennial teens may be shifting back toward more traditional values and may be more interested in following rules than inciting rebellion. But they are also suspicious of packaged messages and highly critical of anything they perceive as hypocrisy. We must be honest with this generation, and what is more, we must be *real*. They want more than communication—they want *connection*. We can't just spout platitudes; we must share our hearts!

Set the stage for real communication.

Long before the curtain parts on opening night for a Broadway play, crews have been working behind the scenes for weeks, setting the stage. Before you try to talk with your teen about sex, love, or dating, make sure the stage has been properly set.

Learn to start speaking their language.

Teens often seem to have a language of their own. They talk of blogs (online journals), bands you've never heard of, movies you don't want to see, video games you don't understand, and friends you've never met. But if you hope to convey the importance of

key point
GET TO KNOW YOUR TEEN.

healthy relationships, good choices, and eternal values, you must commit to investing time in their world.

Learn some of your teen's own personal language, interests, and dreams!

What interests your teen? Where does he or she spend the most time and money? Is your daughter an avid volleyball player? Does your son spend hours trying to master the next level of his latest video game? Be it fashion or football, music or movies, cars or cartoons, learn something about it. Learn enough to talk a little—and listen a lot. Learn enough to show you care.

TARGET MOMENT

You were a teen yourself once, remember? How did you feel when your folks took time to chat with you and share some of your interests?

If you have been a somewhat distant parent in the past, your teen may wonder, "Why the sudden interest?" Go slowly. Don't just plop down on his bed expecting a deep and personal conversation. Try showing up at her sporting events, especially if you have been too busy in the past. It doesn't take much eavesdropping to discover a CD or movie that your teen is into. Even a sincere "How was your day?" can be a great start. Resolve to be with your teen in his or her world whenever possible, and gently look for ways to connect.

THE NAME GAME

Name two of your teen's best friends.

Name one of your teen's teachers.

Name your teen's favorite ice cream.

Name a dream or goal of your teen.

DID YOU KNOW ...

There are a lot of great games that require players to answer dumb questions about themselves. It's a good way to laugh with—and at—each other.

❖ *The Compatibility Game* (Mattel)

❖ *Apples to Apples* (Out of the Box Publishing)

Name your teen's favorite movie.

Name your teen's least favorite food.

I (Karl) happen to be the only male in our household (unless you count Thomas, our 10-year-old neutered cat). Now, to be fair, none of the females in our home would qualify as "girly" girls. But, nevertheless, in order to enter my daughters' worlds, I've endured countless hours of feminine activity— chick flicks, hair and nail moments—I even had my toenails painted once! You get the picture, and we hope you get the idea. Do whatever it takes to connect with your teen. The rewards will be priceless.

Learn to quit speaking and to listen.

Ask any teenager what frustrates her most about adults. Studies show that teens overwhelmingly say that adults "just don't listen enough." That one complaint exceeds all others combined! It is so hard to listen—and listen well. It feels so … passive. But it's not. This may sound like a paradox, but the fastest and most effective way to get your teen to listen to your ideas about dating and sexuality is first to spend time really listening to what she has to say.

key point
TEENS NEED THEIR PARENTS TO LISTEN.

The intimacy of a family meal is a great place to learn about your teen's world. Although today's hurried lifestyle means that families can't expect to share every meal, we need to do what it takes to make it happen as often as possible. The family table is where we can find out how the history test came out, who made the soccer team this year, when the sophomore class is sponsoring their next movie night—and even privileged information like who is going out with whom.

> **Courage** is what it takes to **stand up** and speak; **courage** is also what it takes to sit down and **listen.**
> —**Winston Churchill**

Remember that God gave us two EARS but only one mouth. Maybe that's because we're to do twice the LISTENING!

key point

SHARE TIME ON A REGULAR BASIS.

In our home, family dinners have often been pre-empted by play practice, science-fair projects, and church youth-group activities. For your family it may be sports, dance recitals, and math league. That's all good stuff, but not a good trade-off.

If morning time seems to be more consis-tently controllable for you, one parent can get up a little early to prepare something fun for breakfast, and the family can enjoy time together at the very beginning of the day.

TRY THIS!

Avoid fighting evening pandemonium by having breakfast together. It's a great way to start the day with your busy teen!

Many of the best listening opportunities occur when you are one on one with your teen. Years ago, we purposed to spend several hours alone with each of our daughters every week. During the elementary grades, they enjoyed either of us bringing a small pizza to the school cafeteria for lunch. As they got older, it became walks on the railroad tracks or trips to the coffee shop (our treat). Looking back, we cherish each of those priceless moments. And we think we accomplished the most on the days that *we* talked the least.

5
GREAT LISTENING TIMES!

ON WALKS

SHOPPING

ROAD TRIPS

AFTER SCHOOL

AFTER DATES

Listen to your teen—you'll be amazed how much closer it will make you!

Avoid exasperating your teen.

Remember the challenge of learning Bible memory verses? As kids we usually learned them on the way to church that morning, grateful for the short ones. Usually the teacher was a parent, right? And what parent doesn't want her child learning the principle, "Honor your father and mother … that you may enjoy long life on the earth." (Ephesians 6:2, 3) Sometimes my frustrated dad seemed only half joking when he asked if I really wanted to enjoy long life on earth!

Teens can be a source of real frustration for their parents—and vice versa!

But what about the next verse? It simply states, "Fathers, do not exasperate your children; instead, bring them up in the training and instruction of the Lord." Perhaps that is a passage every parent should commit to memory. As we know, those closest to us can most effectively get under our skin, and the truth is, teens can be time-consuming, physically and mentally exhausting, and quite often frustrating. On the other side, could it be that the way we respond to our teens may often be unintentionally exasperating, annoying, and even infuriating to them?

How you speak means more than what you say!

94% to 97% of all communication is nonverbal.

Unnecessarily harsh tones, lengthy lectures, and discipline doled out rashly in the heat of an explosive moment can all work to close the hearts of our teens and block meaningful communication. Yes, discipline, correction, and instruction are important parental responsibilities, but these must be carried out thoughtfully, prayerfully, intentionally, and appropriately.

If you want your teen to listen and speak respectfully to you, model that same behavior to your teen!

BIG BIBLE POINT

Read Ephesians 6:4 and Colossians 3:21. Then ask yourself the following questions:
• What do I do that might frustrate my teen?
• Am I always in control of my anger and feelings when we talk?
• How can I be more sensitive and less reactive?

❶ Would you let anyone else speak to your teen the way you do? Why or why not?

❷ What if a teacher used the same tone and facial expressions you use when talking to your daughter or son?

❸ What would you say to that teacher? to your teen?

Have you ever had a job where a boss had authority over your work? If so, have you ever made a mistake in the workplace? Most of us have. Now, imagine how you would want your boss to respond to your mistake. How would you want to be confronted? What tone of voice would you prefer to hear? How long would the ideal conversation on the issue run? Your answers to those questions may give you a peek into the heart of your less-than-perfect teen. When he messes up (all teens will), be firm and in charge (after all, you are the parent!), but still treat your teen with the respect and consideration you would like when on the receiving end.

Make your house "date friendly."

It's seldom an overnight accomplishment, but if you want your house to be the hangout for your dating teens, it helps if it was the fun house for them when they were younger kids. Teens are picky about where they want to congregate, so make your home part of their normal "grazing area" as early as possible. If your teen is willing to "have the gang over to the house," then you need to do all you can to make those kids want to come. Wouldn't you rather have them at your place, with your rules, than off somewhere else? Think about it.

Make your house an inviting and welcome spot for your son or daughter to hang out with friends.

key point

MAKE YOUR TEEN PROUD OF YOUR HOME!

"The best way to keep children at home is to make the home atmosphere pleasant—and let the air out of the tires."—Dorothy Parker

Kids don't care overly much about house cleanliness or decor. They *do* want to feel welcomed and comfortable. The teen years are so short—make the most of them !

An owner of a fun house knows teens are more important than carpet and collectibles. Fun houses and hangout houses have good TVs, comfy couches, cabinets with chips and cookies, and fridges with sodas and ice-cream bars. Spontaneous after-school or after-the-game gathering places are part of an active teen's social life. So, instead of worrying about your teen's evening agenda, be in charge of it.

Owners of date-friendly houses provide a gathering place that's not in the middle of other household activities, yet not in an isolated area. If your teen is group dating or solo dating at your house, the rules should still be the same—lights stay on, blankets are not needed (you'll gladly turn up the heat if it's chilly), and some places in the house are off-limits.

IF YOU FEED THEM,
THEY WILL COME!

PARENT TIP

If there is a teen in your house who is not yours, you are responsible for what happens. This includes what movies are watched, how the computer is used, and the actions of that lovey-dovey couple on the couch. Unless your teen is really trustworthy and able to corral the group, it is not wise to go to bed while they are just "finishing up the movie."

We bought our house thirteen years ago and knew it would make a great teen hangout someday. We purchased a ping-pong table and a used pool table. We hung old album covers on the wall and have collected a nice variety of stains on the carpet. But we have met our kids' friends—and we're glad that they feel welcome in our home!

WHAT DO YOUNG TEENS THINK OF THEIR PARENTS' INVOLVEMENT IN THEIR LIVES?

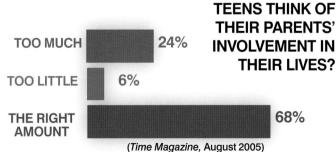

TOO MUCH 24%

TOO LITTLE 6%

THE RIGHT AMOUNT 68%

(*Time Magazine*, August 2005)

SET THE STAGE FOR REAL COMMUNICATION.

The first steps are the hardest.

The first steps are the hardest. You've heard that before, and you know that it's true. The most daunting part of most tasks is the beginning. You know the challenge. You've set the stage. Now is the time to begin.

It really isn't too late—yet.

Some of you bought our first book, *I Want to Teach My Child About Sex* (Standard Publishing, 2005), which is for parents of children ages 3–12, and you've already been talking with your kids about the beauty of God's design for sexuality. But there are also many parents who probably feel a little behind. You may wonder, "Hey, if my kid is a teen, and we haven't even had *The Talk* yet, shouldn't I just leave it all alone?" No. Now is still the best time to get started.

It's never too early or too late to grow closer to your kids—and to communicate with them!

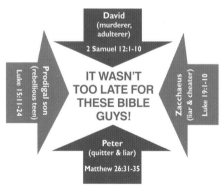

It may not hurt to even joke a little about how you've never had *The Talk*. Laughing at yourself is often an excellent conversation starter with teens. If the topic is going to be awkward or uncomfortable, say out loud that it's awkward or uncomfortable. Your teen will sense it anyway, and you can make progress faster by just owning up to your own embarrassment and moving on.

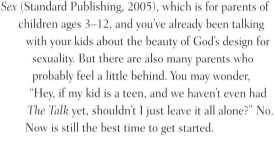

David (murderer, adulterer) 2 Samuel 12:1-10

Prodigal son (rebellious teen) Luke 15:11-24

IT WASN'T TOO LATE FOR THESE BIBLE GUYS!

Zacchaeus (liar & cheater) Luke 19:1-10

Peter (quitter & liar) Matthew 26:31-35

> **"Don't worry that children never listen to you; worry that they are always watching you."**
> **—Robert Fulghum**

In anonymous surveys, teens report that they trust information about sex that they receive from their parents much more than that received from any other source, including the media, peers, or even the medical community. *They want to hear it from you.* Many millennial teens brag with their friends about how close they are to their parents and how they can talk with them about anything in the world. Of course, they won't brag about getting *The Talk,* but they will actually be proud of you if you honestly approach the issue of sex in a conversational, nonjudgmental way.

key point

TEENS WANT TO HEAR IT FROM YOU.

Parents and teens don't always perceive things eye to eye. Check out these eye-openers!

65%	Parents who say they've talked with their teens about sex
41%	Teens who say their parents have talked with them about sex
90%	Parents who believe their teens can ask them about sex
66%	Teens who said their parents are open to questions about sex

(California Wellness Foundation)

During their children's younger years, many parents are afraid to broach tough topics like abortion, masturbation, pornography, and prostitution—but kids will find out about these from their poorly informed friends anyway. All such excuses must be pushed aside now. You have a teenager. He or she already talks about sex more than you probably know. The time to talk is *now.*

Teens admire parents who are willing to bring up awkward topics.

Your role is changing.

Some parents may have purchased this book with the hope that it will provide a healthy, value-based curriculum on teen sexuality that can be taught to their teenage children. It is no simple task to teach matters of the heart. The remainder of this book will provide vital information, but we caution you to impart it with humility, patience, and a willingness to listen to your teen.

key point

GOOD TEACHERS ARE GOOD LEARNERS.

Your teen probably won't respond well if he senses an impending lecture, sermon, or set of regulations presented in condescending tones.

"When I was a boy of fourteen, my father was so ignorant I could hardly stand to have the old man around. But when I got to be twenty-one, I was astonished at how much he had learned in seven years."

—Mark Twain

(from the *Atlantic Monthly*, 1874)

Don't get us wrong. You are the parents—the authority in your home. God has placed your children under your charge. You establish rules, provide leadership, and are accountable to God for the physical, intellectual, emotional, and spiritual development of your children. But issues of sex, love, and dating involve so much more than external mandates. And the looming examinations over this material will not be given in classrooms but within the success or failure of some of the most meaningful relationships your teen will ever experience.

As our kids mature, many parenting techniques that once worked must be set aside. Parenting is a progressive process of teaching, encouraging, and letting go.

At this stage in your child's development, you will often function more as a mentor, coach, or consultant than primarily as a teacher. That's okay. In fact, that is as it should be. When a child is born, we are fully responsible for his safety, nurture, and well-being. But as our children begin to master simple tasks, they should be encouraged to take charge of their lives more and more.

Don't act like you know it all. (You don't, by the way.) We are all in this together. Every day we live, if we can manage to maintain an open heart, we will find that we still have more to learn about relationships.

TRANSFERRING OF RESPONSIBILITY

At birth, parents are fully responsible for their child. As the child gets older, the responsibility becomes less.

In their later teens, kids become more responsible for themselves.

0   5   10   15   20

YOUR CHILD'S AGE

Kids of every age long to feel grown-up. Be careful in broaching the topics of sex, love, and dating, that you do not communicate to your teen that you still see her as a little kid. An ounce of humility may yield pounds of respect!

The remaining chapters of this book can be read by both you and your teen. Laugh together at the silly parts. Think soberly about the challenging parts. Together you can consider God's dreams for your relationships.

Hot Is Cool—Going Out Is In

If you hear your teen say that someone is a "hottie," don't assume the worst. Hottie is a gender-neutral term that means anything from cute to seriously sexy. And the term "going out" is still used—and it still doesn't necessarily mean that they are "going" anywhere. See, our teens are just as weird as we were.

Recognize the classic dating myths.

As parents, we all fit somewhere on the scale between wanting to hide our kids in the attic and trying to push them out the door. So, if your teen isn't interested in dating yet, she will be. And if you think you have Mr. Romance living under your roof, there are ways to rein him in.

Dating is an all-American invention.

Many cultures do not recognize the concept of dating. Life mates for their children are (1) chosen by the parents, with no input from the bride and groom, (2) chosen by the adult child, with parental approval, or (3) chosen by the adult child, with all courting in the presence of a chaperone. Of course, none of that would fly in America! Maybe that's why we have some of the highest teen pregnancy and divorce rates in the industrialized world. Makes you proud, doesn't it?

CHECK THIS OUT!

(50%) 50 percent of today's teens graduate high school without going on a date, yet this generation is marrying sooner, and more often, than others.

No matter what your teen's attitude toward dating, it is still the accepted way eventually to find a mate. Our job as parents is to fit this cultural tradition into the framework of our values and hope for the desired outcome for our children. Dating rules that are established *before the need arises* will greatly decrease the tension of last-minute decisions about who to date and where to go on dates.

LET YOUR TEENS MAKE **DATING RULES** FOR *THEIR* FUTURE KIDS!

- AT WHAT AGE SHOULD DATING BEGIN?
- WHEN DO PARENTS MEET YOUR DATE?
- SHOULD YOU DATE ALONE OR GROUP DATE?
- HOW MUCH PHONE TIME IS APPROPRIATE?
- SHOULD THERE BE TIME ALONE AT THE HOUSE?
- HOW DO YOU BREAK UP WITH SOMEONE?
- SHOULD YOU DATE MORE THAN ONE PERSON?

Most parents want their teens to have a healthy and productive (not reproductive!) dating experience. Do not send your teen out the door and hope for the best—you're still the parent, and she still needs (and wants) your guidance and some boundaries. If you create the rules together, and enforce them with calm determination, your teen will not feel oppressed—she'll feel loved.

Guidance provides freedom—not oppression.

Find the right age for dating to begin.

Where did the idea that 16 is the magical "dating age" come from? Yes, parents need an answer for their 14-(going-on-24)-year-old daughter who wants to go to the movies with a senior! But really, does our child's chronological advancement automatically make her ready to handle the heady (and sometimes "handsy") aspects of being alone with the opposite sex?

Perhaps we should focus less on dating ages and more on the maturity levels of our teens.

It can be very hard on your teen's self-esteem to be *old enough* to date but not be *emotionally ready* to date. Perhaps we should focus less on the age of our teen and more on his maturity level, trustworthiness, and ability to judge character. Does your son understand curfews and dating guidelines? Does your daughter know how to get out of awkward situations? Is your son grounded in his beliefs, no matter what his date may want to do? Is your daughter able to judge a guy's character enough to know if he can be trusted?

10 Rules That Bring Freedom

1. Wait to date.
2. Age differences do matter.
3. No "home-alone" visitors.
4. Always be home on time.
5. Avoid alcohol and drugs.
6. Avoid "at-risk" situations.
7. Watch what you watch & hear.
8. Screen the Internet.
9. Tame the tunes you listen to.
10. Set personal boundaries.

(Bruce Cook, *Choosing the Best*)

You also need to look carefully at your daughter's date. Would you give him your debit card and PIN number or a blank signed check or tell him to take your car? If the answer is no, then why would you let one of your most valued treasures leave your home with a guy you wouldn't even let drive your car? And what about your son? Are the girls calling your house at all hours? If so, your son will probably need your help in handling his hormones—and his pride!

TARGET MOMENT

Do not let the "magical sixteenth birthday," or any other milestone, strip you of all veto power and parental responsibility.

key point

DATING IS A PRIVILEGE, NOT A RIGHT.

> *"It is with our passions as it is with fire and water: they are good servants, but bad masters."*
> —Roger L'Estrange, *Aesop's Fables*, 1692

Trust and levelheadedness do not automatically come with age. Look closely at your teen and your teen's date. Are they ready? The Division of Motor Vehicles (DMV) has created a great pattern for teens getting their driver's licenses. Perhaps teens should earn a "dating license" the same way. The *permit stage* might be when groups of teens go to the movies or out to eat. Then there would be the *intermediate license,* when double-dating at a group event would be allowed. Then, after trust has been proven and good judgment demonstrated, your teen would get a *license to date*—within the boundaries of the house rules, of course.

Group dating is a good starting place.

Let's start with a definition of dating. The school curriculum *Choosing the Best,* by Bruce Cook, defines dating as "any time single people of the opposite sex get together to (1) have fun, (2) get to know each other, (3) try to figure out what they want in a life mate, and (4) prepare for marriage." If that is true, then every time our teens go on a school or church outing, they are dating. Every time a group of kids come to your place for movie night, they are dating. Your teens won't think that church camp or a youth rally is a date, but maybe they should.

key point
THE GOAL OF DATING IS TO HAVE FUN.

Remind your teen that there is safety, more fun, and lots of memorable moments when friends share time.

Group Dating = *All the joys of going out without the pain of breaking up.*

key point
GROUP DATING IS NOT COUPLES PAIRING OFF.

If the goal of dating is to have fun and to know someone better (who might be a potential spouse), the idea of *group dating* is a completely viable choice. When we talk about group dating, we aren't talking about a bunch of couples going out together. We mean that a group of guys and girls, close to the same age, with no pairing off, are just spending time together.

Most kids have more fun in groups because they offer lots of conversation, less pressure, and less expense for the guys. (Who said the guys have to pay for everything?) Also, family dating rules are usually easier to obey in groups. And of all the dating rules that are most often griped about, the dreaded curfew leads the way. You may feel like you are really in control by being inflexible about the magic hour when your teen must be home—but what are teens doing for those four hours before 10:00?

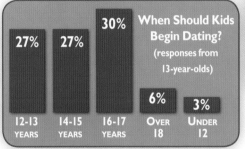

When Should Kids Begin Dating?
(responses from 13-year-olds)

12-13 YEARS	14-15 YEARS	16-17 YEARS	OVER 18	UNDER 12
27%	27%	30%	6%	3%

Source: *Time Magazine,* August 2005

> As a family, discuss the potential positives and negatives of group dating. To make this work, everyone needs to try for an opinion on both views.

Different events need different time limits. A night at the amusement park might run long—so don't demand your teen leave early because the all-important clock is about to strike 10:00! Instead, insist that you be kept informed regarding when, where, who, and what's going on. That's why God allowed the wonderful invention of cell phones!

Group dating is usually more fun, less risky, less expensive, and a more effective way to spend the evening with many more "potential candidates" for a marriage partner.

Whom to date is an important choice!

Near the conclusion of *Indiana Jones and the Last Crusade,* Dr. Jones finally stumbles into the secret chamber supposedly containing the sacred Holy Grail, only to find it hidden among hundreds of imitations. He knows that one sip from the correct cup will bring eternal life, while a sip from any other will result in certain death. The deadpan advice from the guardian knight is, "Choose wisely." No kidding! But still, not bad advice for Dr. Jones—and anyone in the dating years!

Some attractions sizzle and fizzle.

They say that opposites attract and that birds of a feather flock together. So which makes for a better match: differences or similarities? Researchers have tried to answer that very question and have come to the conclusion that both sayings include elements of truth.

> I figure that the **degree** of **difficulty** in combining two **lives** ranks **somewhere** between rerouting a **hurricane** and finding a **parking place** in downtown **Manhattan.**
> —Claire Cloninger

Opposites tend to excite and attract. But it is the strategically important similarities that can help keep a couple flocking together through the years. Religious similarities, intellectual compatibility, and common interests help love grow. Dating relationships built on the excitement and energy of dramatic differences have far less than an average chance of survival. Help your teen recognize (and avoid) the following dating styles.

The first sizzle-and-fizzle dating approach is one that we call "Red Cross dating." It begins innocently enough. You find someone who appears desperately in need of your help, and you feel that you can make a positive difference in his or her life. This person needs help; you need to be helpful. But what happens when he or she needs you less, or (heaven forbid) you need this person for assistance? The Red Cross philosophy is a great way to live but a terrible way to date!

Why do actors and actresses have so many failed marriages? Many have money, fame, and charm but lack good character. They may sizzle at "I do" but often fizzle at "until death do us part."

CHECK THIS OUT!

- In 2000, there were 800,000 American couples with more than 5 years difference in their ages.
- 7 in 100 women married more than once have husbands 6 or more years younger than they are.

(U.S. Census Bureau, 2000)

BAD-BOY, BAD-GIRL

Bad-boy or bad-girl dating is also destined to a disappointing outcome. Sure, it can look like a lot of fun to date someone uninhibited, easygoing, and freewheeling. But bad-boys and bad-girls make lousy long-term partners. Just watch how they treat people (other than you). If most receive very little respect, beware! Your turn is coming soon!

EXOTIC & CHAOTIC

The exotic, mysterious relationship (finding someone exotically different from yourself) and the "May-to-December" connection (someone far older or younger) are two more sizzle-and-fizzle dating strategies. The initial appeal is usually far greater than the staying power. There is nothing wrong with differences in dating, as long as the focus remains on the person you are getting to know rather than on some dramatic quality he or she possesses.

There are always jerks to avoid.

key point

ALWAYS BE KIND— BUT ALSO BE FIRM!

If you've ever seen a scary movie, you've experienced the moment when the lead character is walking right into an obviously deadly situation. Everyone in the theater is thinking, "Watch out! No, no, no!" Some dating relationships seem just as obviously misguided, right from the beginning. There are jerks out there—both guys and girls—and it's our job to help our teens notice and avoid them at all costs.

TARGET MOMENT

Remind your teen that there are immature, selfish people who have growing up to do before they're candidates for a healthy dating relationship.

Most jerks are either attractive, somewhat charming, or both. After all, what has allowed them to stay jerks for so long? Good looks or charisma has probably pulled them out of jams created by their own selfishness for years. Remember that both males and females can have jerkish tendencies.

The Classic Jerk

The classic jerk is extremely self-centered and egotistical. He or she might be an hour late and barely apologize. He may be rude to waitresses or store clerks. She might refuse to meet your family or friends. He may push you to do things you feel uncomfortable doing. In general, classic jerks think so highly of themselves that everyone else pales in comparison. If you find yourself with a classic jerk or jerkette, get out of the relationship as fast as you can.

The Makeover Artist

Another common jerk is the makeover artist. This person enjoys being with you because he thinks you have a lot of potential. (By this he means that, with a lot of work, he may be able to whip you into shape.) He or she constantly criticizes the way you dress, the car you drive, the job you have, the way you fix your hair—even telling you how to look and act. Can you spell R-U-N?

Discuss these quotes with your teen and how they relate to wise dating choices.

"That which is striking and beautiful is not always good, but that which is good is always beautiful."
—Ninon de L'Enclos

"Beauty is indeed a good gift of God; but that the good may not think it a great good, God dispenses it even to the wicked."
—Saint Augustine

OTHER JERKS TO AVOID

THE PARASITE
• with you at all times
• hysterical if you talk to someone else

THE PRINCESS OF EVERYTHING
• expects royal treatment
• demands you read her mind

THE NEEDY SLOB
• wants you to care for him like Mommy
• you pay on the first date

THE SAD PUPPY
• no friends besides you
• threatens to harm himself if you break up

(Marley Pugh, *Life Choices*)

In summary, these kinds of people care much more about themselves than about anyone else. They may occasionally make you feel important, and even be quite attractive and charming, but they also can leave you feeling hurt and embarrassed—and little by little, they erode your sense of independence and self-worth. We're not saying your teen has to date someone who is perfect, but help him or her be honest enough to call a jerk a jerk—and have what it takes to walk away.

WHOM TO DATE IS AN IMPORTANT CHOICE!

Choose from the inside out.

As a kid, didn't you love those stories about great American heroes like George Washington and Abraham Lincoln? Who can forget little Georgie chopping down the cherry tree (not his most ideal "role-model moment") but then quickly recovering when he refused to deny his guilt. *I cannot tell a lie.* Or how about good ol' Honest Abe, who reportedly walked miles in the dark to return a few cents of miscounted change?

key point
CHARACTER ATTRACTS PEOPLE TO US.

95%

86%

95% of Christians and 86% of non-Christians state that they have traditional moral standards.
(Barna Group, 1997)

Remind your teen that character is doing what's right— when nobody is looking.

We loved those stories because they said something about who we wanted to be … and how we still want to live. Character is who you are when no one is watching. Character is what you do when you are certain you'll never get caught. And character matters in dating!

Abe Lincoln said that "character is like a tree and reputation like its shadow. The shadow is what we think of it; the tree is the real thing." What do you think he meant?

As a college psychology professor, I (Karl) have surveyed thousands of students regarding what they value most in dating relationships.

HONESTY AND TRUST ARE VALUED CHARACTER TRAITS!

Responses have included *someone good-looking, a nice figure,* and *the ability to hold a conversation.* Would you like to know the top answers by far? Honesty—and trust. Those were the top two answers, class after class. More students were looking for honesty and trust than any other quality. More than looks. More than money. More than communication. Even more than love.

Ask your teen which of these would serve as a red flag to question the character of a potential dating relationship?

CHARACTER COUNTS!

He has no problem cheating on tests.

She asks you to lie to keep her out of trouble.

He exaggerates his accomplishments.

She won't admit when she makes a mistake.

He makes jokes at other people's expense.

Dave Berry, syndicated humorist, touts an intriguing way to determine the quality of a person's character. If someone makes great efforts to listen cordially and attentively yet is curt and ill-mannered with the service staff, he knows this is a relationship to be avoided. All that glitters is not gold. And all that appears friendly is not necessarily of good character—especially in dating.

BIG BIBLE POINT

Read Romans 5:3, 4 with your teen. Discuss how these traits all lead to solid character and how character forms the basis of our actions, faith, and relationships with God and others.

Consider different dating styles.

Every teen magazine has articles with such titles as "10 Worst Pick-Up Lines," "What to Say on a First Date," or "How to Up Your Cool Factor." Remember your own dating years? No matter how *smooth* you looked on the outside, you were probably winging it, figuring it out as you went along.

Dating takes solid preparation.

What's the best piece of dating advice you've ever heard? Here is ours: *work on yourself first.* Make sure you know who you are and where you are going. Before your teen opens his heart to serious dating relationships, help him search his heart to discover the values, principles, self-awareness, and self-esteem that will set the stage for successful dating.

key point
DATING TAKES GOOD PREPARATION.

key point
ALLOW YOUR TEEN TO MAKE MISTAKES.

Did you ever try to take a class in high school or college that required prerequisites? I (Karl) ran into that hurdle all through my college years. Then one semester, to my delight, an advisor secretly waived the requirements and allowed me to take an upper-level class without the prerequisites. I was in! But after a few weeks, my initial joy was replaced by a growing uneasiness. I was in over my head. I wound up making the only D in my college experience!

All teens have dating jitters, but part of preparing to date is helping your teen learn to take responsibility for her own life choices.

You've probably heard single friends say, "I'm looking for someone to complete me," almost as if they considered themselves to be only half a person while between dating partners. We know the Lord stated that "it is not good for man to be alone," but there is some-thing dangerous in considering yourself incom-plete until marriage.

- **"Do you see a man wise in his own eyes? There is more hope for a fool than for him."**
  —**Proverbs 26:12**

- **"Search others for their virtues, thyself for thy vices."**
  —Benjamin Franklin

- **"The only preparation for that one profound decision which can change a life is those hundreds of half-conscious, self-defining, seemingly insignificant decisions made in private. Habit is the daily battleground of character."**
  —**Senator Dan Coats**

Remind your teen that happiness, security, and fulfill-ment are qualities that grow from the inside out!

Trying to find someone else who will make you happy is an undertaking doomed to failure. The best relation-ships are those between two people who already have a sense of self, worth, and purpose. Two people who can stand alone on their own two feet are able to choose to be together, not out of necessity, but because of a deep, mutual admiration.

Communication styles matter in dating.

It was 1977, my (Karl's) freshman year at Harding University. A new movie, *Star Wars*, was coming to campus, and I knew exactly who I wanted to invite. I picked up the phone and dialed (yes, I rotary dialed) the first six digits of her phone number. As I spun the final number, I paused … my finger holding the rotary disk in place. I was so nervous! I hung up. I tried again with sweaty palms, dry mouth. Only six numbers. I hung up again. It's not easy to talk to the opposite sex!

key point
IT'S NOT EASY TALKING TO THE OPPOSITE SEX.

key point
HOW YOU COMMUNICATE SPEAKS VOLUMES.

Dr. Gary Chapman, author of *The Five Love Languages*, affectionately refers to most women as "babbling brooks" and most men as "the dead sea." Discuss with your teen what these terms mean in relation to communication styles.

How comfortable is your teen in talking with the opposite sex? How much does he talk with anyone? Some parents hope their son will someday utter a complete, intelligible sentence, while other parents dream of the day their daughter will leave for college—and they'll finally get the phone back. Some of this difference is gender-based, but even more of the difference probably has to do with personality types.

It is said that the average male uses 25,000 words per day, while the average female speaks 50,000 words per day … with gusts of up to 80,000!

Introverts and extroverts (of either gender) have very different needs for and tolerance of personal interaction. Extroverts energize themselves through contact and conversation. Introverts enjoy social situations but often become worn-out by a lot of communication. Both the tendencies toward introversion and extroversion are normal,

Everyone has his or her own communication style, and one's not right or better—we're just different!

healthy, and functional. Don't try to break your introverted child out of his shell, nor should you try to dam up one of your "babbling brooks."

HONEST (2 Corinthians 6:7)
NOT HARSH (Proverbs 22:11)
TRUTHFUL (Ephesians 4:15)
NOT DISCOURAGING (Proverbs 16:24)
GENUINE INTEREST (Philippians 2:4)

The Song of Solomon highlights the importance of compliments during the dating process. Check out these other wise ways of speaking to others!

So, back to the question that plagues your teen: *How do you talk to members of the opposite sex?* God's Word has some tremendous advice for how to talk to anyone, and each nugget of wisdom shines brightly when applied to dating relationships. The Lord wants our words to be honest, encouraging, pure, wise, thoughtful, reliable, and appropriate. Bottom line for dating communication? Be yourself. Have fun. And remember that what comes out of your mouth reflects the contents of your heart (Luke 6:45). Everything we say and do should reflect a heart given to God!

CONSIDER DIFFERENT DATING STYLES.

Solid boundaries clarify freedoms.

When is the best time to prepare for a really big project or test? Many of us know the pain of pulling an all-nighter during the school years or burning the midnight oil at work. We've all learned that it's better to plan far in advance and even anticipate distractions that could thwart our goals.

key point
DATING REQUIRES PRIOR PLANNING.

key point
SET SOLID BOUNDARIES BEFORE YOU NEED THEM!

When we plan in advance, our heads are clearer, our thinking is better, and we are usually much prouder of the results. There may be no bigger projects or no more important tests than the ones our teens will face when they make decisions about their own sexual behaviors. When the outcome really matters, it makes sense not to wait until the final moment to formulate a plan.

> When your daughter seems to be sending the message "Leave me alone!" what she's really saying is, "I need you to understand me!" Don't back off. Gently move toward her because she needs you.

Consider the importance of emergency preparedness. No school administrator would wait for a fire or tornado before determining the safest, wisest course of action to take in such a crisis. As parents, we applaud such efforts. When our children's lives are on the line, we do not want to rely on last-minute, poorly designed, haphazard strategies. There is simply too much at stake.

A fire drill may save their lives. A refusal skill may save their hearts.

Each year, my (Shannon's) staff teaches thousands of students how to prepare themselves for the challenges of attraction, dating, love, sex, and marriage. Our program, called "Virtuous Reality," contains an entire section devoted to boundary setting and refusal skills. Working through age-appropriate scenarios, teens get to practice what they would say or do in awkward and dangerous situations.

"A child today faces more sexual signals and temptations on the way to school than his grandfather did on Saturday night when he was looking for them."
—Josh McDowell

Many times students have told us that they have used the actual tools (and words) that we practiced in class.

When is the best time to decide how far to go on a date? When is the best time to figure out whether to say yes or no to an invitation to see an explicit R-rated movie? The answers are obvious: ahead of time, in advance, before you are in the middle of an awkward situation.

Boundaries & the Darker Side of Dating

Remind your teen that many rapes occur during dates. Discuss the fact that date rape is not about miscommunication or temptation. It's about guys who refuse to respect the feelings and boundaries of others. Point out how being prepared and setting up dating boundaries can help.

It's important to help your son or daughter establish boundaries for physical contact before beginning to date. Sexual preparedness involves deciding in advance what kind of person to choose, how far to go on a date, and how to say no if you're in an uncomfortable situation.

It really is worth the wait!

key point
SEXUAL INTIMACY IS BEST SAVED FOR MARRIAGE.

The reasons to postpone sexual activity until marriage are diverse and compelling. New research underscores what the Bible has stated for centuries—that God's ways are not only right but also lead to the healthiest, most well-adjusted relationships. Those who choose to save sex for marriage have numerous benefits to anticipate.

Studies show that choosing to wait leads to a lower risk of divorce, a decreased possibility of extramarital affairs, higher levels of sexual satisfaction in marriage, and overall happier marriages.

60%

27%

Only 60% of 13-year-olds in a recent study thought waiting for marriage to have sex was a good idea—the others with an opinion felt it really didn't matter!

Have you ever read "The Gold Locket" by Robert Wolgemuth? This short story begins with a young man's first significant crush. As Christmas approaches, he looks for a special gift. He chooses a golden locket, and she loves it—but they break up a short time later. Somehow he is drawn to buy a similar locket for his next girlfriend. More girlfriends … more lockets. The story concludes at his wedding, where he realizes how trivial this locket (sexual intimacy) now seems as a gift for his new bride. What a powerful message on the emotional damage caused by premarital sex.

Here's an illustration we often use in assemblies. We cut four long strips of clear packing tape. During the talk, we stick two of the pieces together with the sticky sides. We ask a volunteer to try to separate the strips, but it's impossible without inflicting severe damage on each piece. We then take the remaining two pieces and press and peel them on and off the volunteer's arm several times before inviting him to bond those pieces to each other. They barely stick at all. You can see the wheels turning in each young person's mind when we reveal that the pieces of tape represent people and that sex is intended to glue a couple emotionally to each other. The application is a powerful one: *having multiple sex partners dilutes and trivializes the commitments made in marriage and reduces the ability to bond with a lifelong mate.*

> Like it or not, sex bonds two people together in a relationship intended only for marriage. Outside of marriage, sex carries the baggage of spiritual, physical, emotional, and relational disappointments and pain.

BIG BIBLE POINT

Read aloud Matthew 19:4-6 with your teen. Then discuss the following questions.

❖ What does this passage teach us about being married and the special relationship it becomes?

❖ Why do you think becoming "one" is meant to be saved for marriage?

❖ When God brings two together in marriage, why is no one supposed to destroy the relationship?

❖ How does sexual intimacy before marriage threaten the relationship?

The question "Why wait?" has many convincing answers. And as difficult as it may be to maintain sexual integrity in today's social climate, the spiritual, physical, emotional, and relational benefits derived from waiting will amply reward those who choose purity.

Remind your teen that abstinence reaps great rewards—and the best may be the message that *"I'm worth waiting for!"*

Find men of God and women of faith.

Now and then you find a gem in the most unlikely of places. Asked to present a talk on "Dating God's Way," I (Karl) discovered a 1950s instructional video entitled *Dating Etiquette*. It was hilarious! A 50s-era teen stood at his locker and asked a girl to the school play as a narrator voiced such wisdom as, "Guys, always open the door for your date," "Show up early to spend time getting to know her parents," and "Girls, wait to see what your date orders at a restaurant and then order something less expensive." As the laughter subsided, I asked the women to raise their hands if they enjoyed having a guy open doors on a date. Almost every girl in the auditorium, rather sheepishly, raised her hand.

Don't just look for the right person; *be* the right person!

key point
RESPECT, HONOR & VALUES DO MATTER!

MOST GIRLS APPRECIATE A GUY WHO...

invites her out with details and times.

is willing to meet her parents.

is willing to pick her up at home.

MOST GUYS APPRECIATE A GIRL WHO...

allows him to be chivalrous.

allows him to open doors and help with coats.

lets him pay for the date (at least the first few times).

We may laugh at the old-fashioned, proper-etiquette dating approach of generations gone by, but in some ways today's teenagers long for the respect, honor, and values those days represented.

If you're brave enough, tell your teen some of your own dating stories. He or she will enjoy hearing about the times you thought you were a stud or knew you were a dork. Our girls love hearing about our first dates, our first kiss, the first time we ran out of gas (we really did!). Tell what attracted the two of you to each other. Affirming your spouse in front of your teen gives him a double blessing: it gives him the gift of family security, and it models mate selection skills.

If dating is to be the awesome, enjoyable, affirming experience that God honestly wants it to be, our teens will have to be willing to do what it takes to find (and to be) men of God and women of faith.

I closed that talk with some unusual advice that I'll share with you now. I told the college girls not to look for a Christian guy. Surprised? I told them to look for a man of God. There is a big difference between someone who is just another Christian guy and someone who has *chosen* to become a man of God. I similarly told the college guys not to seek out a Christian girl. Instead, I told them to search for a woman of faith. The difference between a girl who usually goes to church and someone who has dedicated herself to becoming a woman of faith is enormous.

Sex Isn't a 4-Letter Word

Okay. We all agree that sex isn't a four-letter word. In fact, some of us can even say the word in mixed company. But what do we mean when we say the word "sex"? One definition: If any part of your body is in someone else's underwear zone doing anything, you are having sex.

Dispel dangerous myths about sex.

Myth: *something that a lot of people believe but that isn't true.* **Example 1:** You must have a light on when you watch TV, or you will damage your eyes. **Source:** *a lamp manufacturing company.* **Example 2:** *Eating chocolate gives you zits.* **Source:** *moms who keep their chocolate stash from being devoured by their teens.*

Some myths about sex deceive guys.

Teens freely share misinformation and myths about sex, such as: *Boys who have sex are studs,* and *porn doesn't hurt guys.* Remember these myths, for they're still around and still defining "real men" to our teens. Your teen probably knows that women in magazines and movies are not totally real, thanks to silicone and airbrush techniques, but what about the myth of guys who can have sex for six hours straight? I (Karl) have counseled newlywed guys who were convinced that their sexual abilities were completely inadequate because they couldn't perform like the studs in those movies.

Pornography creates myths and sets up unrealistic expectations that no guy (or girl) can fulfill.

MYTHS THAT HURT GUYS— AND THEIR RELATIONSHIPS!

Another myth is that *guys can't control themselves, so it is up to the girl to stop.* Oh please, aren't you so tired of hearing that one? Or how about these two? *The guy is the animal, and the girl is the gatekeeper.* And, *Boys will be boys—but if a girl gives in, she's a slut.* It is imperative that your teen son knows how to respect the girls he dates. Where is he going to learn this respect?

1 GUYS WHO HAVE SEX ARE STUDS.

2 PORN DOESN'T HURT GUYS.

3 GUYS CAN'T CONTROL THEMSELVES.

4 IT'S UP TO GIRL TO STOP.

5 BOYS WILL BE BOYS.

6 IF A GIRL GIVES IN, SHE'S A TRAMP.

TARGET MOMENT

Myths are more than fairy tales—they can become dangerous guideposts for our teens. Help your teen identify and dispel myths and misinformation.

Teen guys learn respect from their dads and other strong role models. Give your son this picture: On any Friday night, your future wife could be out on a date with some other guy. How do you want him to treat the woman of your dreams? So, when you go on that date this Friday, you will likely be with someone else's future wife. Treat her in such a way that you won't be afraid to meet her husband at a class reunion.

Other myths about sex deceive girls.

MYTH 1: MORE BOYS WILL LIKE ME IF I LOOK AND ACT SEXY.

This is true—to a point. If your daughter is allowed to wear clothes that show more skin than sense, she will get a lot of attention, and that could make her (temporarily) very happy. But if she wants to date guys of integrity and wants to be treated as a person instead of a toy, she will be very disappointed. There is one old saying that is not a myth: *Boys date one type of girl for fun but choose a different type of girl for a lifetime mate.* When our oldest daughter, Katie, was in high school, a senior boy told her that he really respected how she dressed modestly. She thought it was strange because he was dating a girl who always showed cleavage. That kind of double talk is what our girls experience every day.

MYTH 2:

IT'S BETTER TO HAVE A LESS-THAN-GREAT BOYFRIEND THAN TO BE ALONE!

key point

SELF-WORTH SHOULDN'T COME FROM GUYS.

Some girls have to have a boyfriend to feel complete or popular. I (Shannon) was always looking for a guy. There is no documentation on this, but in school I was usually more interested in guys than grades. Help your daughter find other interests that increase her self-esteem and add to her knowledge and experience base. If the highlight of her day comes from which guy smiled her way, she's in for heartaches!

MYTH 3: I HAVE TO HAVE SEX (OR ALMOST) TO KEEP A GUY!

This one has been around forever, but the good news is that we are hearing it less and less. Empowering our daughters to know that they can compete for any job and showing them that their brain is bigger than their ovaries will help free them from this myth. After all, using sexuality for gain is called prostitution. A bit harsh perhaps, but if your daughter is desperate to have a guaranteed date and someone who hangs out at her locker, her decision-making skills may need a jolt of reality!

TRY THIS!

As a family, list all the dating myths you can think of. It can be very entertaining, but also enlightening, when you discover a myth that you thought was a truth.

Discuss these myths with your teen. Why are they false?

✦ **By looking at a person, you can tell if he or she has an STD.**

✦ **Love and sex are one and the same.**

✦ **It's better to go ahead and have sex and just get it over with than to wait or say no.**

Teach your daughter to identify myths that put her down or pressure her to "perform." Encourage her not to tolerate disrespect from guys—it's never okay. Remind her that guys quickly learn which girls they can treat in a trashy way!

Sexually transmitted diseases *do* happen!

Teen pregnancy—it's every parent's nightmare. But the odds of your sexually active teen getting pregnant (or becoming a father) are far less than the almost-guaranteed possibility of her or him contracting a sexually transmitted disease.

Viral infections are dangerously catching!

For most viral STD infections, we are talking a lifetime sentence. True, condoms can prevent the transmission of the AIDS virus 85 percent of the time—if used correctly and consistently. (Note the words *if used correctly and consistently*; for more information on that catchy little phrase, go to our website at www.connectioninstitute.com for a clearer definition.) Do the math—that means 15 percent of the time there is no protection from a life-changing or life-ending disease. Is that good enough odds for your teen?

key point
A VIRUS IS A GIFT THAT KEEPS ON GIVING!

✓ **A sexually active girl can get pregnant only 3 to 6 days a month.**

✓ **A sexually active teen can get an STD every day of every year.**

Herpes comes in two forms: **type 1** and **type 2.** The delineation refers to location, with type 1 being *oral* and type 2 being *genital*. However, those lines have become blurred due to the onslaught of oral sex among all age groups, especially among school-aged kids. Herpes is the gift that keeps on giving, and condoms give little to no protection from a disease that is contracted by skin-to-skin contact.

> **TERMS TO KNOW**
> **VD** – Venereal Disease
> **STD** – Sexually Transmitted Disease
> **STI** – Sexually Transmitted Infection

NOT-SO-FUN FACTS
ABOUT HERPES

There is no cure.

Outbreaks can last over 2 weeks.

Painful blisters arise on your mouth or genitals.

You can share it with your partner.

When the sores are healed, you're still not "clean" of the infection.

Medication for treatment is only a suppressant.

You can have it and not know it.

Infection **is a more accurate term than** disease. Diseases **have symptoms;** infections **can go undetected— sometimes for years.**

There are almost a hunded strains of Human Papillomavirus (HPV), but thirty are significant for this topic. These strains can cause genital warts, even cervical cancer. HPV is the most common STD—so much so that the Center for Disease Control does not mandate reporting of positive HPV clients. The good news is that 90 percent of the infections can eventually be overcome by the body's defense system. The bad news is that almost four thousand women die of cervical cancer each year, and 99.5 percent of all cervical cancer is caused by HPV. The worst news is that condoms give no protection against this disease!

One study showed that even among *adults* who knew that their partner already had HIV, only 56 percent used condoms every time!

56% **44%**

Journal of Acquired Immune Deficiency Syndrome

Bacterial infections are cause to worry.

The good news about bacterial infections is that they are curable. The bad news is that the damage they often cause before they're cured is not. Are you getting tired of this whole good news and bad news thing? Well, if we gave you only the good news you'd be happy but stupid about your world. Hang in there and keep your perspective.

key point
THE STD PROBLEM IS ON THE RISE.

It may seem like the end of the world if your teen is diagnosed with an STD, but be sure to keep your perspective. Which would be worse: an STD or ...

- Your teen is diagnosed with cancer.
- Your teen is in a life-changing car accident.
- Your teen is about to become a parent.
- Your teen no longer believes in God.
- Your teen runs away from home, then is arrested for drugs.

The classic bacterial STDs are gonorrhea, syphilis, and chlamydia—hard to spell, not hard to catch. Gonorrhea and syphilis are old-timers in the world of STDs. Julius Caesar and Al Capone both had syphilis, and any war vet can tell you about the unforgettable films that were shown in boot camp about *The Clap* (gonorrhea).

Although 15- to 24-year-olds constitute only one-fourth of the sexually active population, nearly half (48 percent) of all new STD cases occur in this age group each year.

Syphilis starts with flu-like symptoms and chancres (sores), then slowly damages internal organs and the central nervous system. It's treatable if diagnosed in time. Condoms have not been proven to be very effective against the transmission of syphilis.

Gonorrhea and chlamydia are both pus-like infections that love to grow in the dark, moist recesses of the reproductive tract. Although they are both easy to treat, they can cause great damage if left unnoticed—and therein lies the problem. A person can have either of these infections, especially chlamydia, and be totally unaware of the damage that is happening or of the fact that he or she is sharing this disease with every new sex partner.

Are you getting the basic theme here? Social scientists, politicians, and school administrators love to rant about, stress over and condemn teen pregnancy, yet they often almost totally ignore the much larger problem of sexually transmitted diseases. Besides the pain, expense, and embarrassment, there is also a strong chance of sterility, the problem of finding a marriage partner with the same incurable disease, and possibly, death.

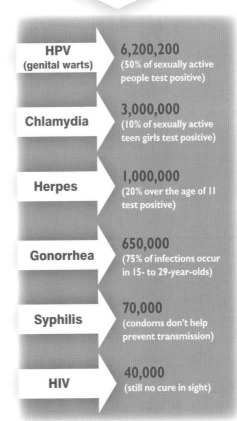

THE **BIG SIX**

Check out the estimated number of new cases annually for these STDs.

HPV
(genital warts)
6,200,200
(50% of sexually active people test positive)

Chlamydia
3,000,000
(10% of sexually active teen girls test positive)

Herpes
1,000,000
(20% over the age of 11 test positive)

Gonorrhea
650,000
(75% of infections occur in 15- to 29-year-olds)

Syphilis
70,000
(condoms don't help prevent transmission)

HIV
40,000
(still no cure in sight)

(Centers for Disease Control, 2003)

SEXUALLY TRANSMITTED DISEASES DO HAPPEN!

Get real about contraceptives and pregnancy.

Now here is a controversial topic: Should teens have access to contraceptives? Should schools be suppliers of them? Should parents know if their teens are using them? Do they encourage sexual activity among the nonactive? Do they really protect the already active from harm? There is a lot to explore, and answers need to be informative—and realistic!

Consider contraceptives carefully.

You've just entered the world of the hotly debated subject of contraceptives and teens. Let us give you a few facts so you can decide for yourself. We have documented every fact, and we encourage you to verify what you read here and what you read anywhere.

CONDOMS

FAILED!

20%

Condoms have a 15 percent failure rate in preventing pregnancy in adults. Two things of note here: we are talking adults, not teens, and we are talking pregnancy, which can only occur during a period of roughly seventy-two hours each month. But what about the condom package that says they are 98 percent effective? The key phrase, once again, is "if used correctly and consistently." Remember, the stated protection rate is for pregnancy, not STDs, for which condoms have a much higher failure rate.

Condom failure rates among teens are close to 20 percent—even after correct usage training!

THE PILL &
THE PATCH

How about the Pill, the Patch, and the Ring? All three of these contraceptives work basically the same way, by controlling the female hormones. All three have room for human error, especially the Pill, but none of them is "the answer to teen sexuality."

THE MORNING-
AFTER PILL

And, of course, we must mention the new controversy, the Morning-After Pill (MAP). This high dose of progesterone must be taken within seventy-two hours of intercourse. It works in the same manner as the Pill, by preventing either ovulation, fertilization, or implantation. Side effects include strong nausea and vomiting, and MAP prevents only 57 to 85 percent of possible pregnancies.

Other contraceptive forms include the following—but are not common among teens and have no protection against STDs.

- IUDs
- sponges
- Depoprevera shots
- contraceptive implants
- spermicides

So what are we saying here, parents? There is no such thing as unmarried safe sex. Come on, how many of your children were planned? How many contraceptive failures are sitting around our breakfast tables? And yet we expect a teen who can't find her homework or remember his gym clothes to "correctly and consistently" use appropriate safe-sex techniques every time? There has to be something better out there than birth control. There is. It is called *parental control*.

Restrictions...

Know what your teen is learning.

There are very few schools in America today that do not broach the topic of sexuality. It sometimes appears in a science class as students discuss the difference between viral and bacterial STDs, or it could appear in a coed PE class, with a purchased curriculum or a guest speaker.

Make sure the school recognizes you as the voice of reason and concern—not as a fanatical naysayer trying to riot the masses!

PARENT POINTER

Frequently, without parental knowledge, teens are taught reproductive basics in biology or health, but they can also be sitting through complete curricula that do not agree with your family values. Be aware. Get involved.

As a parent, you must be aware of what and how this subject is handled in your teen's school. First, ask your son or daughter what is being discussed at school. If you have already established some ease of communication with your teen, this question won't sound like the Spanish Inquisition.

Ask your teen if he has been given any handouts or textbooks. Then ask what your son or daughter thought about the class at school and how it was presented. This will let you know how the class, regardless of the approach, is affecting your teen's perceptions about sex.

Be inquisitive. Be calm. Be firm.

key point

BE AWARE OF YOUR TEEN'S EDUCATION.

If you discover that your junior-high teen is being taught about human sexuality without your consent, then some action is warranted. If you discover that your high-school teen is being taught an approach to human sexuality that conflicts with your family values, then action is warranted. But remember that excessive, righteous indignation will get you little—except a reputation as a troublemaker. Instead, try these suggestions for action.

> Tell your teen about the gross or funny sex-ed classes you had to endure in junior high and high school. It will get communication started—and your teen will love hearing about the teacher who blushed or couldn't even say the "S" word (sex)!

1. Approach the administrators with calm determination. State your concerns, offer alternatives, and bring letters of support as needed.

2. Investigate the sex-education programs of other schools. And check the More Resources list at the end of this book.

3. Offer to find (or to be) an alternate funding source. Some schools use budget restraints as the reason for not changing curricula.

4. Pray and calmly use your persuasion skills. Realize that most schools want the best for your teen!

Make peace with past mistakes.

Is secondary virginity possible? The answer is a resounding "*Yes!*" Secondary virginity is a term that refers to the healing of the heart, the self-esteem, and the reputation of a person who wants to start over. In the physical sense, lost virginity cannot be reclaimed, but in the eyes of God, your child, and a future spouse, it can be.

Secondary virginity is not science fiction.

I (Shannon) was on a flight to Atlanta and got into a conversation with my seatmate. When told him I was headed for a conference to speak on sexual abstinence until marriage, he laughed and said, "So, you're going to a science-fiction convention?" He thought he was so clever! But as I went over my main points (hey, I had a captive audience at 33,000 feet!) he stared at me when I used the term *secondary virginity.* He really thought I was from another planet!

> As **far** as the **east** is from the **west,** so far has he **removed** our transgressions **from** us (Psalm 103:12).

It is not too late to help your teen. No matter what your teen has done (or is doing), there is a way back home—a way to a new beginning. Please, do not give up on your teen! Try to avoid the classic knee-jerk reactions that often add more grief to the situation: (1) giving your teen contraceptives, (2) grounding him from all activities for life, (3) withholding your eye contact or affection to show how hurt you are, (4) blaming your spouse, the school, the church—*everyone.*

You are facing some big issues as a family. Even if there is no pregnancy or disease, the concept of trust is usually gone. What can you do? First, evaluate the conditions that led to your teen's actions. Were the dating rules too lenient, too strict, or not enforced? Is your teen's peer group a positive or negative influence? Is your child trying to fill an emotional void—getting your attention by overt rebellion? You can see by these questions that the possible solution to your problem can be as varied as the reasons behind it.

✓ *Secondary virginity is not science fiction; grace is real.*

Sometimes mistakes are made, remorse is real, and consequences have to be faced. But remind your teen that there *is* a place for healing and a chance to regain what was lost.

Have you ever had a fender-bender or been caught in a lie? Now, does everyone think of you as a bad driver or a liar? Has your teen made mistakes with sexual decisions? Does that mean he or she must always be branded and never start over?

You do not have to face this alone. Find a friend or family counselor to help you sort through your anger and disappointment. Your teen will need to talk to someone as much as, or more so than, you. For the sake of your relationship with your teen, you must move through and past this. It is important to find a way for your teen to feel that he or she has regained your trust. But more important, your teen must realize that he never has to regain your love—for that is unshakable. *Forever.*

There is no sin so great that God's mercy cannot cover it!

Trust your family and church for support.

Sexual integrity that has been lost can be regained. Reputations that are marred can be repaired. But instead of repentance, an erring teen sometimes hides fears behind defiance and seems unwilling to admit wrong choices. And sometimes the erring teen is ready to heal and move on, but the parents or church cannot forgive themselves

key point
FORGIVE OTHERS SO YOU CAN BE FORGIVEN.

or each other. Obviously, if there is no pregnancy, it is easier to work through all the issues as a family—perhaps with outside counsel. But if your teen's sexual activity is known to the community and the church, the healing process holds the potential of being much harder.

What have you done (or would do) if there was a pregnant teen or a young teen father in your congregation? Only if you've always reacted perfectly in such a situation can you expect the same treatment in return.

Parents, you must set aside your pride and embarrassment when your teen's activities become part of the church gossip—or, as some like to call it, *prayer concerns.* Please do not lose sight of Jesus if your church family handles this situation poorly. Remember, the church is made up of people with different understandings of grace and less-than-perfect judgment, and your teen's mistake will, understandably, create some painful consequences.

Do not lose sight of Jesus if your church family handles a tough situation poorly.

> **People who considered themselves to be prolife rose from 33% to 43% in the past 5 years, and those who considered themselves to be prochoice declined from 56% to 48%.**

(Gallup Poll, January, 2001)

Sometimes even believing families consider abortion as an option. At first thought, an abortion would solve so many problems—gossip, shame, and the strain of having to deal with the other teen's parents would disappear. But please hear us: the pain that follows can be so much greater for both the would-be teen mother and would-be teen father. The pain created by sermons or activities that promote life-affirming causes will never go away. Instead of abortion, trust your extended family, your church family, and God to support you through the birth of this child. Whether you opt to raise the child or let someone else do the parenting through foster care or adoption, you'll remember that you chose life for a child.

TARGET MOMENT

Needing to place the blame on a family member, the family structure, or the church because of an erring teen does not heal the wounded.

BIG BIBLE POINT

Read aloud Ephesians 4:32 with your teen. Then discuss the following questions:

• How does Jesus' forgiveness cover us with grace?

• Does it matter if others don't forgive us as long as we have forgiveness in Christ? Explain.

• How does being covered by Christ's forgiveness allow us a new start?

52% of abortions involve women younger than 25.

19% of abortions involve teenagers.

The abortion rate is highest for women ages 18 to 19.

Don't avoid the tough topics.

We've heard people say that the fastest way to kill a conversation is to bring up the topic of religion or politics. But just try bringing up pornography, abortion, dating violence, homosexuality, cohabitation, or masturbation. We're calling these the "tough topics," and we think that each deserves the label. But they're real issues that our real teens will encounter in this real world!

Don't drop the "hot potatoes"!

I (Karl) will never forget being in seventh grade and spending the afternoon at the home of a good friend. The whole family was watching the 5:00 news when a reporter broke a story about a prostitution ring. Unfamiliar with the term, I innocently asked, "What's a prostitution ring?" The room froze. Time stood still. Finally, the father smiled and said, "Why don't you ask your parents?" Good advice.

What does God teach about these hot potatoes? What do Christian leaders recommend for them?

pornography · abortion · cohabitation
dating violence · homosexuality
masturbation

Face it. You are the parent of a millennial teenager, and unless you've been extremely proactive, your teen has probably learned from some other source about porn, abortion, rape, homosexuality, shacking-up, and masturbation. Although you know that each has complex moral, ethical, and spiritual implications, chances are reasonably good that your teen knows little more than what he's gathered from the media and uninformed friends. Many of their beliefs have been shaped by television shows such as *Seinfeld* reruns and MTV. If that sounds good enough for you, go ahead and skip this section. If not, read on.

Your teen deserves to hear the truth from *you*.

DO YOU RELATE MORE TO PERSONALITY A OR B?

A. I frequently love to stir things up.

B. I really don't like to rock the boat.

A. I enjoy speaking my mind even if others don't like it.

B. I prefer moments of harmony when everyone gets along.

If you lean toward A, you probably need to take care not to blow your teen out of the water when you discuss these tough topics. Watch his comfort levels. Do more listening than usual. Take your time. Stop and pray. It doesn't all have to be discussed today. The outcome matters. Do this right.

If you lean more toward B, don't wait forever. You'll never find the perfect time to discuss the hot potatoes. Make yourself speak up. You have information she needs to hear—and she needs to hear it from you. Don't overanalyze every sentence. Take a deep breath, pray, and dive in.

First things first. How well informed are you? You probably have opinions about tough topics such as abortion and homosexuality. Once we're absolutely sure that our opinions are rooted in God, we should gather as much godly wisdom as possible. The rest of this chapter will attempt to at least scratch the surface of the hottest potatoes: pornography, abortion, dating violence, homosexuality, cohabitation, and masturbation. Get out your oven mitts—here we go!

key point

DEFINE YOUR VALUES THROUGH GOD'S WORD.

Pornography is addictive—and dangerous.

Last year I (Karl) began counseling with what looked like the perfect Christian family. Their problem was a very sudden, rebellious streak from "Jake," the seventh grader. In one month's time, his grades plummeted, his attitude soured, and their once-peaceful home became the scene of screaming matches and violent outbursts. Before we had even finished the first session, I found that Jake had accidentally discovered pornography on the Internet. He was ashamed, frightened, confused, and angry. He despised what he was doing, but he continued to feel drawn back to his secret little world. He had begun to hate himself for being perverted (his word) and eventually began to hate everyone around him as well.

key point
PORN HURTS BOTH GUYS AND GIRLS.

CHECK THIS OUT!

60% of all website visits are sexual in nature.
(*Washington Times*, 2000)

90%

Jake is not alone. Jim Burns, president of the National Institute of Youth Ministry, states that ninety-nine out of every one hundred guys have viewed something pornographic, and close to 50 percent of the American teenage population views pornography at least once a month. If you have teenage boys, you *must* have discussions about the serious dangers of pornography.

Percentage of 8- to 16-year-olds who have viewed porn online, mostly by accident while doing homework.
(NOP Research Group, 2002)

Most Christians are aware that pornography is against God's plan. Jesus himself taught us that fantasizing about sexual relations is just as wrong as acting out sexual sin (Matthew 5:28). But few people understand the dangerous, addictive nature of pornography. Often beginning with mere curiosity or an accidental encounter, pornography, much like drugs and alcohol, progressively follows the cycle of addiction. Because of a growing level of tolerance, addicts are compelled to use more and more to achieve the same degree of mood alteration. Attempts to quit are accompanied by the distress of psychological withdrawal symptoms. Eventually, self-deception, loss of willpower, and interference with normal life activities all become part of the addict's profile.

Opportunities to discuss pornography with your teen.

During a Victoria's Secret commercial on TV.

If you see a sign that reads "Adult Superstore."

After a Super Bowl "wardrobe malfunction."

- **Consider a prefiltered Internet service provider such as Integrity Online.**
- **Regularly check the history folder of your browser.**
- **Teach teens never to answer unsolicited emails.**
- **Become informed about addiction recovery resources (for pornography) such as xxxchurch.com.**

Thankfully, Jake wasn't yet deeply addicted to porn. But he did need counseling, accountability, and a strategy for change (including moving the computer to a common room and parents who learned a lot about checking Internet history). But the most important thing Jake needed was reassurance that he was not perverted, that it was okay to talk about his struggle, that he was not alone, that his parents loved him, and that God was eager to forgive him. Talk to your teens about porn, especially your teenage boys. They need to know that the temptation is normal but that the dangers are very real.

Abortion is not a harmless choice.

There are very few middle-of-the-road opinions concerning abortion. Either it is boldly addressed (and usually condemned) from the pulpit, or it is ignored for fear it might offend someone. Therefore, you may know about procedures, laws, and consequences, or you may only know what is presented through the media. There is a good chance, however, that your older teen knows someone who has paid for or who has had an abortion. Still, teens' understanding of the procedures involved may be very limited.

Abortion is not a harmless choice. Discuss your values on this topic with your teen. Arm him or her with equal amounts of truth and compassion.

As of 1999, 29 states had parental involvement laws in effect. But what are the laws in your own state? Use the Internet to stay up to date on the abortions laws in your state.

Although rulings differ in each state, some do allow minor teens to get a legal abortion during any of the nine months of pregnancy. A teen doesn't need parental approval or an accurate medical history in many states, and the father of the baby has no rights—even if the couple is married.

Statistics and controversy usually surround girls and women—but don't forget the impact on guys, who are half the equation. They may not want to choose abortion—or they may *pressure* girlfriends to choose abortion over other choices.

The RU-486 abortion pill is a hotly debated subject. This procedure involves more than just "popping a pill." It's a two- or three-step procedure that can take days, with bleeding lasting for a few weeks. If the procedure does not cause the baby to pass from the girl's body, then a surgical abortion will have to be performed.

78%
of teen pregnancies are unplanned, accounting for about one-fourth of all accidental pregnancies annually.

REASONS GIVEN FOR CHOOSING ABORTION

25.5% want to postpone childbearing.	10.8% feel a child will disrupt their education or career.
21.3% cannot afford a baby.	7.9% want no more children.
14.1% have a husband or boyfriend not wanting a baby.	3.3% are due to a risk of fetal health.
12.2% are too young or parents object to the pregnancy.	2.8% are due to a risk to maternal health.

(Gallup, January 2001)

If your church has over one hundred members, someone in your building has been directly affected by abortion in one way or another.

No girl or woman *wants* an abortion—she only wants escape and a second chance. It's important not to stand in judgment. The physical, mental, social, psychological, and spiritual ramifications are huge for all of those involved. Abortion may be an immediate answer to the crisis problem of an unwanted pregnancy, but it almost always creates much worse problems for years to come.

Dating and violence shouldn't go together.

Just as every teenage boy needs to hear from his parents about the dangers of pornography, every teenage girl must be forewarned about the growing incidence of dating violence. Not surprisingly, the two issues are closely related. Pornography has been proven to objectify women, glorify female victimization, and desensitize men to the horror of violent sexual acts. As the Internet has created an explosion of pornographic availability, the effects of pornography have also increased exponentially. Both our sons and daughters are under attack, and the results are evident in the unsettling statistics on date violence.

key point
DATING VIOLENCE IS ON THE RISE.

key point
DON'T DEAL WITH DATING VIOLENCE ALONE!

8 in 10 teenage rapes are either "acquaintance rapes" or "date rapes."

In the United States, although a rape is reported approximately once every six minutes, the vast majority of rapes are never reported at all. Most of the sexual violence inflicted on teenage girls is perpetrated by someone they already know—and may even be dating. Discussing the following classic scenarios with your daughter will decrease her chances of becoming a victim of dating violence.

CHECK THIS OUT!

There are certain "date rape" drugs that render a victim unconscious and limit memory. Common ones include *Rohypnol, Roofies, Ruffies, R-2,* and *Rope.* These drugs are odorless and tasteless and difficult to detect when put in drinks or mixed with other drugs.

ALCOHOL & DRUG USE

Most sexual assaults and date rapes occur at parties where alcohol is available. Both partners do not have to be drinking to increase the chances of assault. Alcohol is the cause of, or at least is blamed for, most unwanted sexual advances. Date-rape drugs are easily dissolved in drink—even cola—and are hard to detect.

28%
of females who are raped are raped by their boyfriends.

29%
of rape victims are between 12 and 17.

54%
of rape victims are under age 18.

(U.S. Dept. of Justice, 1994)

BEING ALONE WITH A GUY

Until a guy's character is well-established, do not let him take out your treasured daughter alone—he hasn't earned that privilege.

GOING TOO FAR

Unless your daughter has conservative boundaries in the area of physical intimacy, kissing or "making out" may get out of control. If your daughter is in a car making out with a guy on Lover's Lane and he doesn't stop when she says stop, whose fault is it? It is his! But your daughter will still bear the burden and scars of the attack!

Your role in protecting your daughter may easily include becoming a confidant to her friends as well. Let your daughter know that if her friends are in a violent situation, they cannot handle it alone. Prove to your children, no matter their ages, that you can be trusted with secrets they swore never to tell. Some things are too dangerous to remain a secret.

Love the homosexual—hate the sin.

Homosexuality is no longer the taboo topic it once was. Ask middle schoolers what "gay" means, and the impish grins on their faces will quickly tell you they know full well. TV shows (like *Will and Grace* reruns) and movies (like *Brokeback Mountain*), openly homosexual celebrities, and political battles over legalizing gay marriage have kept the topic of homosexuality in the limelight. Our teens know what the term homosexuality means—and it's quite likely they think they understand the subject better than their parents!

GOD'S PLAN FOR SEX =

1 MAN + 1 WOMAN ... 4 LIFE!

key point

TOLERANCE DOESN'T MEAN CORRECTNESS.

The catch phrase of this generation is tolerance—tolerance of all people regardless of race, religion, gender, nationality, and sexual orientation. If your teen attends a high school of more than a couple hundred students, it is likely that he knows someone who professes to be gay. Your teen may even strongly defend that individual's right to choose homosexuality without fear of prejudice or mistreatment. The laws of our country are designed (as they should be) to protect all Americans from unjust discrimination, but here is where some of our teens may be led astray by popular culture.

Just because an activity is protected by law does not make it right in the sight of God.

> "The bottom line is that homosexuality is not primarily about sex. It is about everything else, including loneliness, rejection, affirmation, intimacy, identity, relationships, parenting, self-hatred, gender confusion, and a search for belonging." (James Dobson, Bringing Up Boys)

Adultery is not prohibited by law but is clearly against God's plan. Drunkenness and adult pornography are not against the law, but few would try to argue their virtues. Homosexual behavior is clearly condemned in Scripture (1 Corinthians 6:9) and is described as both unnatural (Romans 1:26) and detestable (Leviticus 18:22). Of course, if we are going to try to fully embrace the heart of God, we must love all sinners and grieve for their sin. The same passage in Romans that calls homosexual activity a sin also lists malice, gossiping, and heartlessness as being equally sinful (Romans 1:26-32). Think about it.

We must be careful to present a balanced, biblical view to our teens as we discuss this issue. Yes, homosexuality is wrong, but no more or less wrong than other

Do you know someone who thinks he might be gay? Tell him about Exodus International, a nonprofit, interdenominational Christian organization that promotes the message, "Freedom from homosexuality through the power of Jesus Christ." Founded in 1976, Exodus has grown to include over 150 local ministries in 17 countries and has helped thousands of individuals exit the homosexual lifestyle. Visit www.exodus-international.org for more information.

sins. No more or less forgivable, redeemable, or changeable than other sins. Our teens should learn from us that even though our world has accepted homosexuality as an acceptable alternative lifestyle, God still says that it is wrong. And we may need to learn from our teens the godly arts of patience, kindness, and appropriate tolerance.

Cohabitation does more harm than good.

*We are **committed** to **each other**—that's why we're moving in **together!***

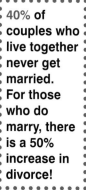

You may snicker at sayings such as *"getting the milk without paying for the cow,"* but if your older teen or adult daughter chooses to live with her partner instead of getting married, the milk will quite likely sour—and you will have one sad Bessie on your hands! The justification for this lifestyle choice sounds so logical to them—and maybe to you as well.

> By **living together** first, we can **see** how we'll get along when we are **married**.

40% of couples who live together never get married. For those who do marry, there is a 50% increase in divorce!

As parents, you need to know what you believe and why you believe it in order to disarm those myths. So here is the truth: your child will do great damage to the existing relationship or to possible future relationships if he or she chooses to move in with a partner. Period.

Three-fourths of children born to live-in couples will see their parents split before they reach age 16, compared to only one-third of children born to married parents.

> **Who** would **buy** a car **without** a good **test drive?**

1 Cohabitation increases young people's acceptance of divorce.

2 Cohabiting couples report lower levels of happiness, sexual satisfaction, and faithfulness than married couples.

3 Women in cohabiting relationships are more likely than married women to suffer physical and sexual abuse.

4 Married couples live longer, are more financially stable, and have better health than cohabiting couples.

(National Marriage Project, 1999)

Judith Treas and Deirdre Geisen, in their article "Sexual Infidelity Among Married and Cohabiting Americans" (*Journal of Marriage and the Family,* 2000) found that affairs are twice as common among couples who live together than for married couples.

Check out the probability of a split within 5 years for live-ins versus marrieds!

49 percent for live-in relationships.

20 percent for married couples.

(National Center for Health Statistics, 2002)

"People tend to romanticize what it [living together] will be like. The fact is, there is a lot of work involved, the same need for communication, compromise, sharing and making sacrifices that married couples face."

—Stacy Whitman

Of course you will love your child, no matter what his decision on this matter—but your teen also needs to know your feelings. You may approve of your child's partner, but that doesn't change the real probability that cohabitation will be harmful to the health of the relationship.

Don't over- or underreact to masturbation.

So, now we've finally arrived at the hottest potato of all: *masturbation*. You think it was hard to talk about porn or dating violence? Try bringing up the issue of masturbation to your teen. But the odds are great that your teen will experiment with masturbation before he or she exits the teen years and will experience diverse emotional reactions as a result. Though this generation probably is not worried about "stunting their growth" or "going blind," your teen still may be haunted with questions like, *What's the matter with me? Does anyone else struggle like I do? Is this against God's will?*

key point

AVOID OVER-REACTING.

key point

HELP YOUR TEEN FIND ANSWERS.

"No form of sexual activity has been more frequently discussed, more roundly condemned, and more universally practiced than masturbation."
—*The Encyclopedia of Sexual Behavior*

The Bible is conspicuously silent on this issue.

Experts convey a myriad of views on the subject of masturbation, calling it everything from immoral to being in the same category as head-scratching to a gift of God. Though Scripture speaks frequently about sexual sin, even listing specific deviancies, masturbation is never even mentioned. It seems wise to us to avoid delineating rules in areas where God has chosen not to speak. There is good psychological evidence to support the belief that occasional masturbation is a normal part of most teens' growth and development.

51%

of Christians favor the idea of making it illegal to distribute movies or magazines that contain sexually explicit or pornographic pictures (Barna Group, 1997). Since masturbation and pornography often go together, it's wise to reinforce the dangers of pornography!

The Bible is not silent about the issue of lustful thoughts, and frequent masturbation is almost always associated with sexual fantasy and pornography. Powerful chemical reactions in the brain during orgasm are intended by God to fuse together a man and wife as one flesh (Matthew 19:5), but outside of marriage, sexual experiences frequently yield dangerous results. Lustful masturbation is highly addictive and often sets the stage for sexual difficulties later in marriage. Because of addiction tolerance, the prolonged practice of masturbation creates the need for increasingly graphic stimuli in order to achieve arousal.

MYTHS ABOUT MASTURBATION

It makes you go blind. FALSE!

It leads to insanity. FALSE!

It is a form of self-abuse. FALSE!

It's a worse sin than rape, incest, or adultery. FALSE!

It's always a big deal. FALSE!

It's never a big deal. FALSE!

The growing acceptance of erotic imagery in mainstream popular culture makes it difficult for any of us to remain pure of heart. Help your teen guard his or her heart, eyes, and mind. Don't make too much out of normal, developmental, sexual self-exploration, but do help create an environment in which such experiences will not be fueled by a bombardment of lustful images.

The person who is most cautious to "set before my eyes no vile thing" (Psalm 101:3) is least likely to be drawn into sexually addictive behaviors.

Forever and Ever— Amen!

Most people will be married sometime during their lives and intend it to last forever. But we all know not everyone lives happily ever after. When is it time for dating to get serious? How can you be sure that the one you are dating is (or isn't) the one? And what does it take to make sure a marriage will be a lasting love?

All you need is love—or is it?

Forty years ago the Beatles asserted, *"All you need is love."* Sounds good, doesn't it? But of course, it all depends on how you define the word *love*. What kind of love did Jim Morrison (of The Doors) have in mind when he penned the words, *"Hello, I love you, won't you tell me your name?"*

Learn the differences in the *four loves.*

Love is such an "all-purpose" word. On any given day, someone might say "I love my dog," "I love ice cream," and "I love you." The ancient Greeks devoted four words to its description. The first is *eros,* from which we derive the English word *erotic.Eros* is the part of love that most people call "chemistry." The second love is *philia,* which you may associate with the name of the city of brotherly love: *Philadelphia.* When you love someone with *philia,* you admire his or her better qualities and enjoy many shared interests and experiences.

> **"The Eskimos had fifty-two names for snow because it was important to them: there ought to be as many for love."**
> **—Margaret Atwood**

LOVE TIMES 4

EROS	"CHEMISTRY" LOVE	This love involves strong attraction and is fueled by sexual energy and hormones.
PHILIA	BROTHERLY LOVE	This is love characterized by friendship, conversation, and interaction.
STORGE	FAMILY LOVE	This is "blood-is-thicker-than-water" love.
AGAPE	SPIRITUAL LOVE	This is Christ's all-accepting, selfless love for us. This is "until-death-do-us-part" love.

Good dating relationships embrace all four types of love!

The third form of love, *storge*, is most often seen in family relationships. This long-term loyalty stands the test of time, various trials, and life's challenges. The final Greek word for love, *agape*, was considered to be more powerful than any other form of love. *Agape* love involves the concept of voluntary commitment. This is "for better or worse" love; it lasts through rich and poor times, through sickness and health.

Agape love comes straight from the heart and soul. This love is a *decision*—a gut-it-out-even-when-you-don't-really-feel-like-it kind of love. This love stands the test of time!

Love at first sight can blind you!

Cinderella's big entrance at the ball left the prince with his mouth hanging open and ready to spend eternity thinking only of her. Snow White's first introduction to her prince was when his kiss awakened her from an enchanted sleep. He scooped her into his arms and carried her off on a white horse to live happily ever after. The Little Mermaid (Ariel) saw a handsome young man through murky waters and knew at first sight she should sacrifice her life, her family, and her voice to be with him forever!

> **key point**
> **LOVE IS A CONSCIOUS DECISION.**

98%

Studies show that more than 98 percent of Americans will be married sometime during their lives, and most who marry intend for it to last forever.

> *"Lots of people want to ride with you in the limo, but what you want is someone who will take the bus with you when the limo breaks down."*
> **—Oprah Winfrey**

Does anyone really believe in love at first sight? You'd be surprised. Few people try to defend fairy-tale versions, but a surprising number of people still want to hold on to the romance of the idea. Music, movies, and literature reflect and shape the beliefs of a culture. Look at the popular songs and movies that promote the love-at-first-sight myth. Just in the last few years, European pop singer Kylie Minogue and rap artist Mary J. Blige have written songs entitled "Love at First Sight."

The healthiest and longest lasting relationships have strong elements of all four loves. *Eros* can ignite a relationship, but it is *philia* that keeps you close through the years. *Storge love* creates the comfort of a family environment, but it's *agape love* that carries you through the toughest times!

Discuss these quotes with your teen and how they reflect that love isn't instant but requires hard work over time.

💜 *"A successful marriage requires falling in love many times, always with the same person."*
—Mignon McLaughlin

💜 *"Gravitation is not responsible for people falling in love."*
—Albert Einstein

The city of Las Vegas has more wedding chapels than cafes. Some of them even have "drive-throughs"! Those quick-marriage chapels stay in business because so many people truly want to believe in love at first sight. They hope the power of love (which in most cases is eros) will keep them together forever. Sadly, but predictably, these relationships usually end poorly.

Obviously, *eros* is unpredictable and sudden, whereas the other loves grow more slowly with time and investment. Not only can *eros* erupt at first sight; it can also be extinguished just as quickly. If love is something you can fall into, it is also something you can fall out of. *Real* love is something you grow into over time.

Remind your teen that love at first sight is almost always about initial magnetism and physical chemistry (eros).

True love doesn't guarantee *happily ever after.*

Remember the movie *The Princess Bride*? (It's become somewhat of a Christian young-adult classic.) The recurring theme of this comedy is true love. Wesley was brought back from the dead (or at least "mostly" dead) by the power of true love! Movies and popular culture make it seem that true love is something mysterious, elusive, and extremely uncommon—and something only young, extraordinarily attractive, incurable romantics can ever hope to achieve.

key point
TRUE LOVE ISN'T ABOUT PERFECTION!

HONESTY—99%

LISTENING—98%

RESPECT—98%

GIVING—98%

Men's and women's responses when asked to check words describing the qualities of true love.

TENDERNESS—96%

The *true love* myth can create some very real problems, especially through the expectations it generates—expecting never to argue, never to experience tough times, never to need space, or never to be (even slightly) attracted to someone else. Help your teen realize that, not only are most of those expectations unrealistic, unattainable, and unmaintainable, but many of them would not be healthy even if they could be fully realized!

SEX—75%

DIGNITY—64%

LOGIC—50%

PRIDE—44%

(*Oprah Magazine*, February 2004)

Only about 12 percent of formerly married people thought they would ever get divorced.

WHY ARE YOU BREAKING UP?

- **The #1 reason cited by males is *incompatibility*.**

- **The #1 reason cited by females is *lack of maturity*.**

(Dinah S. Temple, *Picking Up the Pieces,* 2005)

But if wanting to eat at the same restaurant tonight is evidence that a couple is experiencing true love, what does it mean if tomorrow they disagree about which movie to watch or where to go after the show? Couples that over-emphasize the importance of shared beliefs, thoughts, and interests often become unnecessarily disappointed when either of them diverges from the common path. The subtle belief that true love will insulate you from frustrating disagreements can set couples up for failure. If two people both have their brains turned on, they will naturally experience different opinions and approaches.

True love is more about acceptance than perfection.

A fairer test for true love would be to measure a couple's ability to disagree without sacrificing either honesty or kindness. The apostle Paul set the bar high when he instructed us to "speak the truth in love" (Ephesians 4:15). Remind your teen that true love takes effort, compassion, and loads of patience!

> "Marrying for love is a fairly recent phenomenon," says Charles T. Hill, psychology professor and co-author of the *Boston Couples Study.* "Until 150 years ago, marriages were arranged in this country, and in many places they still are. The idea that marriage needs to meet psychological needs, that your spouse should be your best friend, that's an idea invented after 1950. Making that the cornerstone of marriage is a whole new perspective."

It's not always easy to tell if this is *the one*.

Ask almost anyone how you can tell whether or not the person you're dating is *the one*, and the answer will most likely begin, "Well, if he (or she) is, you'll just know it." Then you'll likely be told that, when you really love someone, something inside you will tell you this person is different. Thanks a lot! That really helps!

Finding the *right one* can be confusing.

We've already discussed the frustratingly broad definition of love. Maybe it would help more if your friend were to ask what kind of love you feel for this person. Do you feel *eros, philia, storge,* or *agape* love? Teens are often in love with the idea of being in love—yet wonder if what they're feeling is love. Sound confusing? Imagine how your teen feels in trying to sort it all out!

key point
LOVE CAN BE VERY CONFUSING TO TEENS!

The majority of the world's population believes itself to be in love at any one time—but many more women than men desire to be in love!

HOW MUCH TIME DOES IT TAKE TO FALL IN LOVE?

The majority of both female and male respondents under 30 say 3 to 6 weeks is enough time to fall in love!

What do people mean when they talk about being "in love"? Most teens have a very personal version of what love is or should be. There may be a way in-love couples are supposed to look at each other, feel in each other's presence (and absence), talk, touch, and relate. It's not uncommon for someone to see a young couple and proclaim, "It sure is easy to tell they are in love!"

All those signs are an important part of the *eros* side of being in love. You may recall the romantic montage near the beginning of the movie *Shrek II,* as the newlyweds enjoy their honeymoon vacation on the beach to the sounds of the song "Accidentally in Love." But the most important elements of a lasting love happen far from accidentally. Help your teen understand that *agape* love infers and demands conscious decision making. This love truly is a choice and involves the mind as much as it does the heart.

STOP & CONSIDER

"Nearly all marriages, even happy ones, are mistakes: in the sense that almost certainly, in a more perfect world, both partners might have found more suitable mates. But the real soul-mate is the one you are actually married to."
—J. R. R. Tolkien, in a letter to Michael Tolkien, 1941

Rather than asking, "How do I know whether or not I'm in love?" a better question might be, "Is this someone worth choosing to love?" During the dating process it is wise to be extremely selective, to fully engage the thinking, choosing side of love. The next few pages will help in the process of sorting through the most important considerations and making the best choice possible.

TREAT CRUSHES SERIOUSLY!

"Parents tend to view teen romance as practice for the real thing. But to your child, this is 'it,' " says author Ritch Savin-Williams (Cornell University). To help, you can try the following:

- **Don't jump quickly to give advice.**
- **Listen supportively & carefully.**
- **Let your teen process feelings.**

Kissing for one minute burns 4-6 calories— but it takes a lifetime of minutes to realize true love!

Establish your gotta-have-its and deal-breakers.

If you gave your son or daughter a gift certificate for a music CD, what would he or she buy? Most people have strong preferences about the type of music they enjoy. What would you think if your teen took the gift certificate to the mall and picked a CD simply by choosing the one with the most attractive cover art—without regard to likes or dislikes in the music itself? What are the chances your teen would be happy with his choice?

Discuss these quotes with your teen. What do they teach us about marriage, its value, and the hard work involved?

"People try much less hard to make a marriage work than they used to fifty years ago. Divorce is easier."—Mary Wesley

"The success of a marriage comes not in finding the 'right' person, but in the ability of both partners to adjust to the real person they inevitably realize they married."—John Fisher

Some people put more thought and planning into their music choices than they do into their dating choices!

"Don't marry the person you think you can live with; marry only the individual you think you can't live without."—James C. Dobson

Your son may know exactly what type of CD he would look for, but has he seriously considered what type of girl is worth his time pursuing? Your daughter might be appalled to find a country (or rap or rock) CD in her car, but has she considered that there are a number of young men she should be appalled to even consider dating? And what about those who select dates because of their "cover art"? How wise is that?

We strongly believe that anyone who is dating should thoughtfully and prayerfully create two lists: a list of "gotta-have-its" and a list of "deal-breakers." *Gotta-have-its* are the essential qualities someone must have in order to even be considered a serious dating option. *Deal-breakers* are the characteristics that must be avoided at all costs.

WHEN SHOULD YOU BEGIN DATING?
(according to 13-year-olds)

(*Time Magazine*, August 2005)

54%		
	30%	
		6%
12-15 YEARS	16-17 YEARS	OVER 18

10 GOTTA-HAVE-ITS	10 DEAL-BREAKERS
good work ethic	irresponsibility
real communication	moodiness
kindness	smoking
sense of humor	pornography
intelligence	anger
parenting skills	greed
honesty	arrogance
trust	jealousy
attractiveness	gambling & addictions
spirituality	recklessness

Help your teen determine the "non-negotiables." After all, no one wants to experience "buyer's remorse" in dating—or later in marriage!

Before dating begins, encourage your teen to invest the time, thought, energy, and prayer needed to write out these two lists of qualities. It's very affirming to see your well-thought-out convictions in print, and compiling the lists will put your teen well on the way to recognizing whether or not someone is worth dating—or eventually marrying!

Teach your adult child how to say "yes."

Bet you thought you were done with *The Talk*. Bet you were thinking, "We raised him well, taught him how and who to date, got him engaged. My job is over." Well—almost. There is just one last bit of advice that your adult children will need. See, you have taught them how to say no to sex all these years—now it is time to teach them how to say "yes."

key point

THE TALK ISN'T OVER YET!

WHICH WOULD YOU CHOOSE?

HAVE A TAX AUDIT.

LOSE YOUR HOUSE IN A TORNADO.

HAVE 4 ROOT CANALS ... WITHOUT NOVOCAINE.

PREPARE YOUR ALMOST-MARRIED CHILD FOR THE HONEYMOON EXPERIENCE!

✔ **Consider a marriage seminar for your soon-to-be-married child and his or her partner. They can calm fears and often answer questions that the couple may have.**

Before our adult kids even get close to being married or having their own homes to care for, we feel obligated to teach them the basics. The basics of how to make a budget, how to plan and cook a meal, how to heat water in an electric skillet when they forget to pay the gas bill.

If we give such sound advice for other areas, why do we hesitate to advise them on having a great married sex life? The obvious answer is, *Who wants to talk to their children about how to have sex?* But perhaps you are misunderstanding our point. Someone, somehow, needs to mentor your soon-to-be-married child on the sexual aspects of the honeymoon, and it doesn't need to be a peer bearing tales of unexpected terror or indescribable joy.

Your newlywed offspring and his or her mate will be more willing to work on their marriage right at the beginning than at any other time. Do all you can now to help them off to the best start possible!

99%	**Percentage of couples who take a honeymoon**
7-9	**Number of days in a typical honeymoon**
$4,000	**Average cost of a honeymoon today**

Guys and girls are both equally curious, equally hopeful, and somewhat fearful of unstated honeymoon expectations. What do they ask? They have the same classic questions you had: *Is it going to hurt? How will I know what to do? What if my spouse is not pleased with me?*

"Love takes up where knowledge leaves off."
—Saint Thomas Aquinas

Help your soon-to-be-married child find answers by sharing your own experiences or helping locate resources that are useful and informative.

Let the experts help inform your teen.

Our friend Troy tells the best "before-I-got-married" story. He was 23, and it was the night before his wedding. The whole family was at his parent's house, and Grandpa told Troy that he wanted to have a little talk with him. Now, Troy has great respect for his grandfather, but he really didn't want to have *The Talk* with him. Troy and his bride-to-be were virgins, but he was certain they would be able to figure out everything. Anyway, Troy did go on a walk with Grandpa, but Grandpa wasn't talking. Then, after about twenty minutes, Grandpa stopped, turned to Troy and said, "Son, sex is better at 73 than it ever was at 23!"

> **Love** is the **word used** to label the sexual **excitement** of the **young,** the habituation of the middle-aged, and the **mutual dependence** of the old.
>
> —**John Ciardi**

When we tell that story to high-school students, they all yell, "Gross!" But it proves our point: *the most important sex organ is the brain, and the second most important is the heart.* The other things are just really nice extras that make baby-making a lot easier—and more fun!

If it's hard to talk with your older teen or soon-to-be-married child about married sex and commitment, let the experts speak for you!

There are a lot of great books out there designed for the just-about-to-be-married crowd. Your child will greatly appreciate a gift from these three suggestions.

1 *Intended for Pleasure* (Rebell Publishing, 1997), by Ed and Gaye Wheat, was "the book" when we were newlyweds. But don't worry, it's not so old that it talks about dinosaur sex—it has been updated three times since then. This book has separate chapters for husbands and wives and sections on birth control and sex during pregnancy. It even has chapters on sex after you reach your 60s, 70s, and 80s.

TARGET MOMENT

Instead of another set of plastic storage bowls, make sure the newlyweds get a subscription to Marriage Partner magazine! (See More Resources)

2 *Sheet Music* (Tyndale House, 2003), by Kevin Leman, is one of our favorite books on this topic. The book is designed for soon-to-be-married-couples to read the first four chapters *before* the wedding night and the rest of the book later. With chapter titles like "Too Pooped to Whoop," this book is straightforward, funny, and a definite conversation starter.

Our favorite marriage seminar (besides our own) is Tommy Nelson's on the Song of Solomon. His seminar is not sappy and mushy—but hard-hitting, engaging, and always well-received by both genders.

3 *The Act of Marriage* (Zondervan, 1998), by Tim and Beverly LaHaye, is another good pick. Tim LaHaye is certainly leaving no one behind in this classic book on the beauty of sexual love. With over two million copies sold, the LaHayes must have figured out something!

Let your teen grow up—then let go.

key point
EVERYONE HAS HIS OWN IDEA OF LOVE.

What sounds romantic to your teen? An evening stroll on the beach? Candlelight dinner for two? Your son or daughter probably has a vision for what constitutes love, romance, and commitment. Recently, as we were discussing special memories, Shannon caught me completely off guard. She told me that one of the most romantic things I ever did when we were dating was a time when she was sick with the flu and I held her hair back into a ponytail as she threw up into the toilet. She added that it was in that moment that she felt more loved than ever before!

> **Love is when the other person's happiness is more important than your own.**
> —H. Jackson Brown Jr.

DID YOU KNOW?

You're 35% more likely to become ill if you're in an unhappy marriage. Encourage your teen to choose carefully—for his life and health!

What made that a special memory? That little act symbolized something important to her. It meant that I was committed to the relationship. To her, that moment stands out as a turning point in our relationship. Now, twenty-five years later, it's all more clear than ever. Commitment is the key. We hope that you have that kind of marriage. And we know that you dream of that type of relationship and marriage for your own sons and daughters.

Prepare yourself. Someday your teen son or daughter will be in a dating relationship that will begin to grow into something more. We know that, in your eyes, your daughter's scraggly boyfriend will never be good enough for her (or you), and your son's sweetheart may never be able to meet all of your standards — but the day will probably come when he or she will choose to leave the nest.

"When mothers talk about the depression of the empty nest, they're not mourning the passing of all those wet towels on the floor, or the music that numbs your teeth, or even the bottle of capless shampoo dribbling down the shower drain. They're upset because they've gone from supervisor of a child's life to a spectator. It's like being the the Vice President of the United States."
—Erma Bombeck

We hope that when that time comes you will have been talking with your child for years about sex, dating, love, and relationships and, as a result, will be reasonably certain that he or she has chosen well and is adequately prepared for a healthy marriage. It will then be time for the healthy steps Jesus described as leaving and cleaving (Matthew 19:5). Let your child grow up. We hope that by then you will have worked yourself out of a job—for that was actually the plan all along.

key point
LET YOUR TEEN GROW IN HEALTHY WAYS.

key point
CELEBRATE EACH DAY WITH YOUR TEEN!

More Resources

BOOKS

for teens

- Stephen Arterburn and Fred Stoeker, *Every Young Man's Battle* (WaterBrook, 2005).
- Henry Cloud and John Townsend, *Boundaries in Dating* (Zondervan, 2000).
- Sean Covey, *The 7 Habits of Highly Effective Teens* (Fireside, 1998).
- Willard F. Harley Jr., *The One: A Field Guide to Relationships That Last* (Zondervan, 2001).
- Eric and Leslie Ludy, *When God Writes Your Love Story* (Multnomah, 2004).
- Neil Clark Warren, *Date or Soul Mate?* (Nelson, 2002).
- Ben Young, *The 10 Commandments of Dating* (Zondervan, 1999).

for parents

- D. Ross Campbell, *How to Really Love Your Teen* (Cook Communications Ministries, 2003).
- Gary Chapman, *The Five Love Languages of Teenagers* (Northfield, 2005).
- Keith Deltano, *Fighting Back: How to Promote Abstinence in a Sex-Saturated World* (Freedom Entertainment, 2004).
- Les Parrott, *Helping the Struggling Adolescent* (Zondervan, 2000).
- David Scherrer and Linda Klapacki, *How to Talk to Your Kids About Sexuality* (Cook Communications Ministries, 2004).

WEBSITES

- www.helpguide.org/index.htm (expert information on emotional wellness that will last a lifetime)
- www.christianteens.net (Christian chat, an online youth pastor, a teen message board, and more)
- www.bebroken.com (an online leader in sexual-addiction resources, with an emphasis on promoting biblical purity)
- www.christianitytoday.com/teens (solid dating advice, help for living out your faith, articles about TV shows and movies, personal stories from other students, and recommendations for cool Christian music)
- www.connectioninstitute.com (Virtuous Reality abstinence program and contact information for Shannon Wendt)
- www.firepower.org (a site for connecting teens grades seven and up)
- www.lifeteen.org (resources and training that encourage teens to grow in their faith)

Subpoint Index

Chapter 3: Sex Isn't a 4-Letter Word 46

Chapter 4: Forever and Ever—Amen! 76